How to
a Self-Help
Book

Successful techniques for creating a guide
that transforms your readers' lives

GINNY CARTER

First published in Great Britain by Practical Inspiration Publishing, 2023

© Ginny Carter, 2023

The moral rights of the author have been asserted.

ISBN 9781788604628 (print)
ISBN 9781788604642 (epub)
ISBN 9781788604635 (mobi)

Every effort has been made to trace copyright holders and to obtain their permission for the use of copyright material. The publisher apologizes for any errors or omissions and would be grateful if notified of any corrections that should be incorporated in future reprints or editions of this book.

Want to bulk-buy copies of this book for your team and colleagues? We can customize the content and co-brand *How to Write a Self-Help Book* to suit your business's needs.

Please email info@practicalinspiration.com for more details.

To my mother, Jenifer. I never knew you but this book couldn't have been written without you.

Contents

What you'll get out of this book

You're a coach, a therapist, or a trainer – an expert who helps people to feel happier in some way. You work with your clients one to one or maybe as a group, and you're wanting to broaden your impact so that you can transform more lives. Of course, there are various ways of doing that, but one in particular stands out. It's accessible to anyone who needs your advice, it's easy to pick up and put down, and it's low in cost. It also, as it happens, has the potential to change your life at the same time. That way is to write a self-help book.

Why is having a book such a useful tool? For a start, you can reach many more people with a book than through face-to-face work. And those people are ready to buy your book, because the self-help market is growing each year. In the UK, for instance, self-help guide sales have recently risen by 20%.[1] When someone has a problem they often look for a book to help them solve it; wouldn't you like yours to be the one that they choose?

[1] www.theguardian.com/books/2019/mar/09/self-help-books-sstressed-brits-buy-record-number

There's also the boost to your professional status to take into account. If you've written a book, it means that you must know your stuff – it's an impressive achievement. And because it elevates your status and increases your authority, new and better opportunities come your way. These could be speaking engagements, more people wanting to pay you to help them, and professional collaborators seeking to tap into your new-found reputation. It's as if, instead of working within four walls, you now do it out in the open. You're no longer your clients' best kept secret, but a valuable resource with whom lots of people want to work.

There's another amazing thing that happens when you write a book about your knowledge and understanding: you find yourself developing more of it. This is how creating a self-help guide can become a vehicle for your own professional improvement. Writing in depth about anything changes you, because when you have to explain yourself in a way that others can understand, you come to a deeper realization of your own expertise. Ideas and connections pop up that you'd never have seen otherwise, and you find yourself having the space to really think about what you do.

Finally, writing a book allows you to put your stamp on your work. You know that framework you developed three years ago, which has been helpful for so many clients? Now that it's recorded in a published book, it's irrevocably yours. The same goes for all the other ideas, models, and diagrams that you use to describe your thinking. You're making your expertise tangible, because a book is something that people can hold. In that way, you're creating a legacy both for yourself and your profession.

So, it seems like a great idea to write a self-help guide, but here's the thing. Your book will only help your readers, raise your profile, and deepen your understanding if you go about it in the right way. Unfortunately, many personal development authors don't do this, and in my experience this is down to three key mistakes.

- **Instruction:** instead of working *with* their readers, they *tell* their readers how to think and what to do – this doesn't work.

- **Missing links:** they don't translate their advice into actionable steps, so readers are left with theory but little practice.

- **Modesty:** they don't make their expertise clear, which means that their readers might not trust their advice.

Let's look at these in turn. The first – telling readers how to change rather than working with them – is the single biggest issue that I come across. It's as if the authors of these books are standing on the sidelines directing their readers, rather than putting their arms around their shoulders and leading them to a better place. This is the main reason why a lot of self-help books don't have the effect their authors would have wanted.

Why is it a problem? Because nobody makes a fundamental change to their life on account of someone telling them to do it. As Lisa Cron explains in her excellent book *Story or Die*, 'even the most rational, objective pitch to change your behaviour still tacitly implies you're doing something wrong in the first place. Why else would you need to change? Plus, who wants to be told what they should be doing? People don't change because you tell them to. You gotta wanna.'[2] I imagine that you've seen this with your clients. You know what they *should* be doing to create a transformation in their lives, but it's not as simple as

---

[2] L. Cron, *Story or die: how to use brain science to engage, persuade, and change minds in business and in life* (2021), 4.

just describing it to them. To create a lasting shift, you have to communicate it in such a way that doing it becomes the only option that makes sense. Why would it be any different in a book?

The challenge can be that, when you're used to helping people by talking with them, the tried and trusted techniques that work so well in person don't always translate onto the page. You're left wondering how to communicate your ideas to your readers so that they're felt by them inside, rather than just understood intellectually. The good news is that there are various ways of doing that in a book, and it's the theme that runs through this one like a golden thread. You'll learn how to develop trusting relationships with your readers so that they're willing to walk alongside you on their path to change.

The second issue of missing links – not translating theoretical advice into actionable steps – is also a stumbling block for many self-help authors. When you work with people face to face, you naturally blend the giving of information with the teaching of how to put it into practice. After all, if your clients don't have a way of making use of what they've learned, the process is only half complete. But in a book, it can be trickier. You can't ask your readers what they've understood and what they haven't, nor can you talk them through the steps they need to take in a way that's specific to them. You have to find a way to do that in writing instead, which is something you'll discover how to do here.

The third issue of modesty – not emphasizing your credentials and experience – is one that I think stems from the reluctance of many self-help authors to 'bang their own drum'. It's understandable, because when your work revolves around helping people in a sensitive way, you're naturally reluctant to make it about you. It's all about your clients and their needs.

The problem with this comes when you're asking people to trust your advice in a book. They can't read your body language or look you in the eye, so they're reliant on what you tell them about yourself on the page. Building this kind of trust from scratch might not be something that comes naturally to you, but there are ways of doing it.

To practise what I preach, let me tell you a little about myself. I've been a ghostwriter and book coach for ten years, specializing in self-help guides, business books, and memoirs. I work with all sorts of brilliant experts who want to make an impact on the world with a book, but either don't understand where to start or have given up in frustration part way through. The wonderful thing is, I know exactly what they're missing, and when I share this with them it changes everything. My job is to make sure that every book I work on delivers what its author wants, both for themselves and for their readers, so I've spent a lot of time analyzing what makes a clear and persuasive book. Not only that, but my 18 years' marketing experience prior to my ghostwriting career taught me about strategizing and promoting books; doing this is essential if you're to write the right book for the right readers and market it in the right way.

My experience with personal development guides was intensified during my regular stints judging a set of book awards. I was twice a judge in the personal development category, which meant that I read nearly 100 self-help books in short succession. Some were excellent but many were unconvincing, which was a shame. The ones that didn't work so well left me feeling unsure about the author's advice, nor could I see what the next steps were for me as a reader. I certainly wasn't impacted by the experience. This judging process gave me a strong feel for what makes an effective self-help book and what doesn't, and I've brought what I learned into the one that you're reading now.

My goal is to give you everything you need to write an excellent self-help guide that will do justice to your ideas, expertise, and knowledge. In the first part, 'Define your book', we go through how to set your strategy. You'll decide what you want to achieve with your book, what you'll write about, who your readers are, and what kind of self-help guide yours should be. In the second part, 'Outline your book', I walk you through how to plan and structure your book so that you take your readers from problem to solution in as convincing a way as possible. The third part, 'Write your book', is when we delve into the fascinating art of clear and persuasive writing; this is where you avoid the 'telling not persuading' trap that I mentioned earlier. And in the fourth part, 'Put your book out there', you'll learn how to edit, publish, and market your book; this is what makes all your effort worthwhile.

You'll see that, throughout this book, I use the analogy of a journey. That's because the process of taking someone from problem to solution is like accompanying them on a trip. The first part of writing a book is to decide what kind of journey you're setting off on, the second part is planning it out, the third part is actually going on the trip, and the fourth part is reaching your destination. I'm your tour guide – the saviour who's going to take you under their wing and lead you to your destination. It doesn't matter if you've only just arrived in a strange land without a clue how the place works, or if you've been there for a while, kicking your heels and not sure where to go next. Let's pack our bags and head off on a journey that will equip you to write the personal development book that changes your readers' lives forever.

DEFINE YOUR BOOK: CHOOSE YOUR JOURNEY

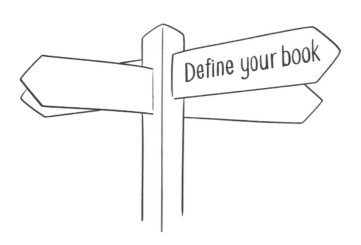

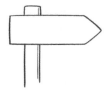

1. Your aim

One of the things that I love to do when I'm visiting a strange city is to wander. If I have no destination in mind, or any kind of agenda, it's amazing what treasures I can stumble across. My favourite discoveries have been an ancient stone fountain as I walked around a random corner in Granada, a couple in full wedding regalia who were posing for a photographer in Beijing, and an exquisite, snow-covered square in Prague that I hadn't expected to be at the end of a long, narrow alley. I should also add that I'm well-known among my family and friends for becoming easily lost (although, sometimes having no sense of direction can be an advantage).

However, exciting as it can be to trust to serendipity when travelling, when you're writing a book, it pays to have a plan. The benefits of this are threefold.

You write a better book. You probably have a good idea of who your book is for and what you want to write about; maybe it's a guide for people who want to lose weight, or feel more confident, or be better parents. That's a great start, but there's so much more that you need to know if you're to write a self-help guide that hits its mark. This is one of those things that's difficult to understand until you do the planning in practice, so please trust me for now; after you've read this part of the book, you'll see what I mean.

It takes you less time. Writing three chapters only to realize that you have too much to say in the second one, and that part of the first one should go later in the book, and that – aargh! – you don't have enough material for the third one, is the bane of any author's life. It's time-consuming and frustrating to embark on a mammoth copy-and-paste exercise that could have been avoided if you'd thought through each chapter beforehand. Plus, it's quicker to write about your points if you know what they are to begin with.

It's easier. It's not the writing that's hard, it's the switching. The analytical thinking you use when you're deciding what to say uses a different set of mental muscles to the creative thinking that you employ for writing your first draft. It follows that your brain is used more efficiently if you do one task and then the other. If you keep chopping and changing between the planning and creative writing, you'll feel more tired and disorientated than if you do the planning first.

That's not to say there isn't room for a little wandering as well. Who knows what ideas and inspiration may come around the corner when you least expect them? Embrace them when they appear because that's part of the fun of writing a book. But be clear with yourself that these are exceptions to the rule, and that they're all the easier to incorporate because you have a solid structure in place already.

What does creating a plan for your book involve? That's what this part of the book will walk you through. Each of its four chapters is based on a fundamental decision that will shape your book and influence what you'll get out of it when it's published:

- What you want to achieve with your book
- Who you're writing it for
- What it's about
- What kind of book it will be

These are four seemingly simple commitments that can hide a wealth of opportunities, because they give a depth and purpose to your book that making it up as you go along will never do. Instead of creating something that's yet another guide to 'x', you'll write one that could become the must-read book in your field. Let's look at each of the four in turn.

What you want to achieve with your book

The first decision is the most critical one, because every other decision you make will hang off this. You're working out the end destination for your book here – the results that you want to get from it. This will affect who you write it for, what it's about, what style and format you use, how you publish it, and how you market it when it's done. So, quite a lot then.

What do I mean by 'achieve'? It's the value that you want your book to give to the following:

- Your readers
- Yourself
- Your business

Your readers

You help people for a living, so deciding how you want your book to change your readers' lives is a great place to start. Thinking about the work that you do with clients for a moment, what's the transformation you offer them? If you find that question hard to answer, another way of looking at it is to ask yourself where they are when they first start working with you compared to where they end up – the journey you take them on. Here are some examples of what I mean:

- From feeling confused about relationships to knowing what they want
- From feeling tired all the time to brimming with energy
- From arguing with their children to living in a harmonious household

What's the fundamental change that you provide? From what to what?

Once you have that, try to be more specific by condensing your readers' destination into one word. The benefit of this is that it will help to keep you laser-focused on what you want for your readers throughout the process of writing your book. For instance, in the examples above, the destination for the first could be 'clarity', the second 'energy', and the third 'harmony'. I appreciate that your clients probably gain more than just one thing from working with you, but I encourage you to be simple for now. Out of all the things you give them there's bound to be one that's the most important – the thing that sends them away happy and that they recommend you to other people for. Focus on that.

Yourself

Let's turn to you. What do you want your book to do for *yourself*? It's important that you pinpoint this because writing a book is a long and sometimes hard-going project, and there may be times when you'll be tempted to give up. You need a clear benefit for *you* if you're to stay the course. Given that your work involves focusing on other people's needs, it might be a challenge for you to do this, so here are some ideas to get you going:

- I want the satisfaction of having written a book
- I want to be recognized as a true expert
- I want to be respected by my professional community
- I want more people to have heard of me
- I want to leave a legacy

Your benefit may be one, more, or none of these, but if you don't know what it is, you won't be able to make sure that your book delivers it for you. And you'll find it a lot harder to stay motivated when you feel too tired, busy, or distracted to keep writing. On the other hand, when you're clear about the personal boost you're going to receive, it's amazing what a powerful nudge it can be to keep your fingers moving across the keyboard.

Your business

I talk to a lot of people who are thinking about writing a self-help book. Sometimes they want my help, either through me ghostwriting it for them or coaching them to write it themselves; sometimes they just want to chat through their ideas. They all share one thing in common: they gloss over what they want the book to achieve for their business. Because although you may think of yourself as a coach or a therapist, you're also a business owner. You're going to be putting lots of your precious time and energy, which could have been spent with clients or on other ways of earning a living, into writing this book. So it had better be worth it, right? Here are some ideas to get you started:

- I want to attract more clients
- I want to raise my rates without worrying about my bookings dropping off
- I want more, and paid, speaking opportunities
- I want to be able to pick and choose my clients
- I want to sell more spaces on my training programmes
- I want to fill my workshops more easily

Please don't feel bad about this – it's completely reasonable to make money from your book in these ways. Not only is it necessary for you to get something out of it for your business, but it's also in service of you spreading your message more widely. You'll be helping more people, in more areas of the world, than if you stay in your little box working only with those you reach through your current means. It's a good thing.

This is a helpful moment to expand upon the point I made earlier about the planning of your book making it a better one. If you're clear with yourself about why you want to write a book in the first place, you will:

- Know what to write about (something we'll explore in Chapter 2)
- Choose the best angle or 'take' on your topic (ditto)
- Know who to write it for (Chapter 3)
- Create a book structure that works for your desired outcome (Chapter 4)
- Pick the most appropriate publishing option (Chapter 11)
- Do the marketing that puts your book in front of the right people (Chapter 11)
- Generate the highest return on your investment (Chapter 12)

Without an end destination in mind, you'll struggle to make the decisions that will best serve your book in all these areas. Of course, you may achieve great results without the advance planning, but it would be through luck, which seems like an unreliable way to spend several months of your life. You'll be more likely to end up at the place you want, as well as encounter some fun adventures along the way, if you have what you want to achieve top of mind.

Is this book-writing project starting to seem a little more appealing now? Can you feel your motivation rising as you contemplate the payback on your investment? In the next chapter we'll explore that all-important topic: what you're going to write about.

The landmarks

If you want to write a ground-breaking self-help book that's relatively quick and easy to write, there are four decisions to make before you begin:

- What you want to achieve with it
- Who it's for
- What it's about
- What kind of book it will be

When deciding what you want your book to achieve, you need to think about:

- Your readers
- Yourself
- Your business

2. Your topic

Your book is based on a journey which starts with the key problem that your readers have and ends with them implementing the solution to it. You're the guide for them on that journey, helping them to understand their challenges more clearly and give them the support they need to overcome them. So the topic of your book is encapsulated in what the journey is – it's the very essence of it.

That might sound simple, but when you're writing about a subject you have in-depth knowledge of, it's surprisingly easy to go off track. There are so many ways in which you can approach it, and so many elements you can include, that what could be a clear and helpful guide to overcoming a particular issue might become a catch-all for everything you know. Your book ends up sinking under the weight of its own information, which isn't useful for your readers. Luckily, there are techniques that you can learn to avoid this.

The one thing

The first method is to limit your book's topic to one key idea. There are three reasons for doing this:

- **It helps to get your book noticed.** People browsing bookshops and online bookstores find it easier to choose a book if it's about one striking proposition than a whole bunch. One idea is concrete and simple to grasp, but five ideas make it hard for them to come to a decision. That's why product brands put their resources into attracting customers for one key attribute: we buy Andrex® toilet paper because it's 'soft and strong', and Nike trainers because they'll help us to 'just do it'.

- **It makes your book talked about and recommended.** Do you remember the last time you saw a TV series you loved? When you discussed it afterwards with your friends, did you give them a blow-by-blow account of the intricacies of the plot? Or more probably, did you say something like, 'It's about a girl who goes to live with her estranged father, and they end up turning each other's lives around.' It's the same with books. Readers love to talk about and recommend one easy-to-express idea, so don't make it difficult for them.

- **It gives your book more value.** We humans find it tricky to absorb multiple ideas at once, which is why a book that hangs off one clear idea will always make more of an impact than one that tries to do too much.

Let's see how this could play out in practice. Sarah is a therapist who specializes in helping people with depression to move through it and come out the other side. She's writing a book because she wants to help more people than she can work with one to one, and also because she'd love to break into the speaking circuit at conferences. She's pretty clear on what she wants to write about, but when she starts thinking about it she becomes drawn towards other mental health issues that people with depression often have, such as anxiety and social phobias. Surely, she thinks, if her book is to be super-helpful, she should cover off these at the same time. However, if I was working with Sarah, I'd steer her away from that because her book should address the *one key problem* that her readers have, and no more.

It's the same for your book. The reason for this lies in the difference between how you see your expertise and how your reader sees their problem. For Sarah, it's easy to expand from talking about depression to other mental health issues because she has pre-existing knowledge of the relationship between the two, but for her reader it's not. In their mind they have one barrier to happiness, which is that they feel depressed; they're not thinking about anything else right now. They may find it helpful to learn about related topics once they've addressed their core issue, but not in the same book. If Sarah tries to cover off too many things at once, she'll end up confusing them. Wisely, Sarah decides to focus her book on the subject of depression and save anxiety for her next one.

The right thing

Your book should be about one thing, but it should also be about the right thing. Sarah's book is about how to work through depression, but the problem is that it's still too wide a topic and she's not sure that her core idea stands out. There are many books on the subject already, which means that her readers will need a compelling reason to buy hers. This is where she needs to unearth what I call the 'gold' in her book – the crux of what it will be about. It's her specific solution, put across in her own special way.

How do you find the gold in your book? There are several ways.

Discover what makes you 'you'

The gold in your book is the same as the gold in you – the way you help your clients that's uniquely yours. What is it? You might find it helpful to think back to what clients tell you has been most useful about your work. It could be a combination of your personality, your expertise, your background, and anything else that makes you 'you'. If you'd like to explore this more deeply, I can recommend the book *Find Your Thing* by Lucy Whittington; it helps its readers to pinpoint their 'thing' and is also an example of a personal development guide that's a joy to read.

Ask what works you up

Your strongest opinions can be your most reliable guide to the gold in your book. What trap do you see your clients falling into time and again, which could so easily be avoided? What frustrates you most about how your peers and competitors do their work, and that you think isn't working? What's the one thing that people always get wrong? These feelings are pointing to what makes your perspective different. For instance, what frustrates me most when I read some self-help books is when the authors tell their readers what to do rather than working with them to help them change. That's why this book is geared towards steering clear of that pitfall.

Decide your 'even if'

Let's say that you're a career coach and you're writing a book about how to switch career in mid-life. You could give information on how to do that, but your readers don't want the obvious answers. What they're really keen to know is how to switch careers *even if* they've never worked in the new field before, or *even if* they can't move to a new location, or *even if* they don't want a drop in salary. The 'even if' bit points to your gold because it's what your readers are looking for over and above the standard advice. I once ghostwrote a book that was about how people can get on with others *even if* they violently disagree with them; this unlocked a whole new world for its readers. Think about what your own 'even if' could be.

Focus on your core expertise

Sometimes, the most obvious factor is the one that gets missed, which is to write your book about the thing that you know best. If you do that, not only will it likely be a good one but you'll probably have an audience for that topic already, which will make marketing your book easier when it's published. The main reason that some people don't do this is because they're lured by the attraction of exploring new fields; this, they assume, will be far more interesting that what they already know. If you find yourself going down this path, think carefully before you carry on. Do you know enough to write a whole book about such virgin territory? Do you have ways of reaching a willing readership for it? If the answer to either of these is 'no', you may regret your decision later. This is so important. I come across many authors who've spent months writing the wrong book – the one that they assumed was based on the best topic, but which was actually just the one they happened to be most excited about, or which they thought would make them look most impressive. Of course, it's a good thing to be enthusiastic about your subject, but you need more than that to create a book that will sell.

These methods will help you to dig out the 'gold' in your book idea, but how do you know whether your topic will make your book noticed, talked about, and valued? In other words, what will your readers think of it? There are a couple of questions you can ask yourself.

Does it put across a distinctive point of view?

If you want your book to make a difference, it needs to put across a novel or unique perspective. Two books that have done this successfully are *The Power of Now* by Eckhart Tolle and *The One Thing* by Gary Keller. Tolle puts forward the idea that the present moment is all that matters and explores the world-changing implications of that viewpoint. Keller outlines the case for achieving more by doing less and narrowing your focus. Neither is the first person to have written on these subjects but the way they present their arguments, along with their particular take on them, makes their books special.

It's also worth bearing in mind that if your book offers a distinctive take on your area of expertise, it will almost certainly divide opinion. While you may not set out to alienate people, not everyone will like or agree with your book – and that's okay. It comes with the territory of saying something worthwhile.

Does it flip a switch?

You know that black-and-white picture of an old woman with a big nose who, depending on how you see her, suddenly turns into a young woman (or is it the other way around?). Something that you assumed was one thing now appears to be another, and no matter how many times you look at it after that, you can never see it in the original way. Similarly, the book idea that takes your reader on the right journey should cause them to hold a whole new set of opinions on their situation by the end. It should help them to turn the old woman into the young one, or vice versa, just as if a switch has been flipped.

The competition, the context, and the craving

In addition to unearthing the gold in your book, there are three further aspects of your topic to consider. These are to do with the environment it will be published in and the mindset of the readers you're aiming at. I call them the three Cs:

- The competition
- The context
- The craving

The competition

I was once on a video call with a book coaching client when he raised a concern. He was writing a book about breaking free from drug addiction and was worried that it would end up being yet another volume about the subject. Turning to the bookshelf behind him, he lifted up a stack of competitor titles. 'Look at this lot!' he said. 'And this is only a selection of what's out there. How will mine stand out from the crowd?' I paused for a moment. How could I put it? 'But see,' I replied. 'You've *bought all those books* and read them yourself. Of course, you're an expert in drug addiction so you want to research what other people have written, but your readers won't limit themselves to one book either – they'll want to read more. Your book will be your take on your topic, so it's always going to be different to anyone else's.'

Worrying about the fact that there are other books already published about the same subject as your own is one of the most common reasons for would-be authors to give up before they've started. I'm here to tell you that it shouldn't be. And, if you're still wondering whether you should add to the already groaning bookstore shelves in your field, ask yourself this: *How many cookery books do I own?*

In fact, it's only if no one else has written a book in your field that you ought to feel worried, because that suggests there's not much of a demand for it. When you look at it like this, your competitors are actually your supporters. For instance, a quick Amazon search throws up over 70,000 results for books about losing weight. That might seem like stiff competition (and it is), but it also shows that there are potentially millions of people interested in reading about the subject. Some of them appeal to some readers, and others to others. They each have their place, just like your book will.

The context

When you're thinking about your core topic, it's helpful to envisage the context that it will sit in. For instance, many books have been written about the 'three principles', a psychological and spiritual explanation of where our experiences come from and how things are created in the world. One of these books is *A Little Peace of Mind* by Nicola Bird, which explores the understanding in the context of resolving anxiety. Another is *The Little Book of Big Change* by Amy Johnson, which explores it in the context of breaking unhelpful habits. And another is *The Relationship Handbook* by George Pransky, which explores it in the context of developing satisfying relationships with the people we love. The underlying concepts are the same between the books, but the contexts are different.

This matters, because when readers come to a self-help guide they're obsessed with their own personal contexts:

- I want to feel confident when I walk into a roomful of people. *The context here is social interaction.*
- I'm desperate to stop arguing with my husband. *The context here is intimate relationships.*

- I'd love to enjoy my job instead of feeling stressed by it. *The context here is work and careers.*

The context may be narrow or broad, but to your readers it's all that exists. At the point at which they're thinking about buying your book, they're only interested in whether you can solve their specific problem as they see it playing out in their lives, so your task is to make sure that your core topic is context specific. What's your context?

The craving

Think of the last time that you spent money on something. It was either on an item that you *needed*, such as groceries for your kitchen cupboards, or an item that you *wanted*, such as a meal at a restaurant. These are the only two reasons that we buy anything.

For most people, it doesn't matter how much they might *need* a book, for them to buy it they have also to *want* it. Let me give you an example. Suppose you help people to spend more of their time doing what they love by showing them how to become organized at work; less time spent working means more time with their families. You know from experience that the readers you're aiming at don't get excited about the idea of being organized, but they do like the prospect of having more free time to enjoy.

Your book will be about learning to be organized, but that's not the idea your readers are most attracted to. It would seem like a drag to them, right? How do you get around that, given that to win the free time they need to learn organizational skills first? The answer is that you make your book the one that people *want* to buy. You do that by structuring the content wisely, choosing the right cover design, title, and back cover blurb, and by marketing it in a way that focuses on that end benefit:

the enjoyment that people will gain if they follow your advice. You'll learn more about this as you progress through the book, but for now it's worth bearing in mind that what your book is about isn't necessarily the thing that will make it sell.

In the next chapter, we'll explore the other side of the topic coin: your readers, and what they want to learn about.

The landmarks

- Your book should be about one thing and one thing only.

- It should also be about the right thing: the topic that gets your book noticed, talked about, and recommended.

- Unearth the gold in your book – the element that makes it irresistible to your target readers.

- Other elements that affect the topic of your book are what else is on the market and the context in which your book will solve your readers' problems.

- Your readers' wants, rather than their needs, have an impact on how you present your topic to them.

3. Your readers

In the first chapter, we talked about what you want your book to achieve for your readers, yourself, and your business. We explored what transformation your book will give to people – the things that they'll be able to do and the way that they'll feel after they've read it. It follows that to write a book that takes your readers through this change, you first have to know them intimately. Because a book that's written for 'everyone' will appeal to no one, whereas a book that's aimed at one set of people whom you completely understand, will sweep them off their feet. In other words, you're asking yourself not just what journey you're going on with your self-help book, but who with.

Be selective

Imagine that you're standing in the foyer of your local cinema on a Saturday night. There's a hustle and bustle around you, the buttery scent of popcorn is wafting past your nose, and you're excited about the evening ahead. But what to watch? You glance at the posters on display. There's an action movie starring a guy sporting big muscles and a torn vest; a romantic comedy featuring a dippy-looking couple with the Eiffel Tower behind them; a psychological thriller with five serious men in suits; and a foreign language film, the main character of which appears to be a middle-aged woman in a red dress.

You'll make your decision based on your personal preferences and experiences. If you've previously been bored by action movies and rom coms (may I raise a hand here) you'll probably skip past those and plump for one of the other choices. But if tucking into a box of Maltesers while devouring a good old love story is something that you know will make you happy, the rom com will be all yours.

What does this have to do with book readers? It's that film producers identify and analyze their customer groups so closely that they can predict what they'll enjoy even before it's hit the screens. Your readers also belong to a group with shared traits, preferences, and experiences. Your job is to identify what those elements are so that you can write the book that's irresistible for them. What could those things be?

Your readers' problem (as they see it)
If you're writing a book about how to communicate effectively, your readers are those people who find this a challenge. But it's not enough for them simply to have trouble with their communication skills – heaven knows, we could all do with some help with those – they must also have a *view of themselves* that tells them that this is what's holding them back. That means your book should be aimed readers who are frustrated by their shortcomings in this area rather than everyone who has that problem.

This is an easy distinction to miss. If you don't get it right, you'll write a generic book that will be aimed at pretty much everyone, rather than for those who are committed to improving their communication skills. Not only will this affect the content, but also the way you present it. Remember when we talked about writing a book that people want, not need? We all *need* to improve our communications, but only a subsection of us *want* to. Those who recognize that they have a problem *and* want to do something about it are the readers you're aiming at.

Your readers' desires, goals, fears, and frustrations

To write a book that speaks to your readers, you need to be familiar with their inner drivers for buying and reading it. Jon Morrow is a blogging expert whose advice I've often found invaluable, and much of his wisdom is just as relevant for book writing as it is for short form pieces. He advises writers to focus on the obsessive thoughts that are troubling their readers. These can be split into two types: positive motivators (desires and goals) and negative motivators (fears and frustrations). These can also be categorized by whether they're ongoing or time-bound, as you can see here:

	Ongoing	Timebound
Positive	Desires	Goals
Negative	Fears	Frustrations

Desires, goals, fears, and frustrations

Desires and fears are usually ongoing conditions; someone may yearn to feel more fulfilled in their work or be afraid of feeling lonely. Goals and frustrations, on the other hand, are time-bound. A goal is something positive that a person wants to achieve and once done will usually stay that way, such as finding a permanent partner. A frustration is something negative that's causing them pain right now, such as being in debt.

This distinction can be helpful when you're thinking about what state of mind your readers are in before they start your book. Are they:

- Desiring something that will take them a long time to achieve, if ever?
- Afraid of something that might never be banished from their lives?
- Aiming to achieve something that they can then remove from their to-do list?
- Frustrated by something that they want to rid themselves of right now?

What's top of mind for them? It could be all four, but they probably have one driver that's more important than the others.

Also, we're not just talking about any old desires, goals, fears, and frustrations, but those that have special qualities. For your book to be irresistible to its readers, it needs to be written for those who are struggling to solve their problems in a big way. They have desires, but they're ones that they can't imagine they could ever satisfy. They have fears, but they're ones that they worry will never be eradicated. They have goals, but they're ones that seem impossible to achieve. And they have frustrations, but they're ones that they can't see a way to be free of. These aren't trifling issues, they're high-stakes games.

They represent the difference between 'improving your career' and 'loving your job forever', or 'losing weight' and 'not dying young'.

I know what you might be thinking. *This seems a bit exploitative to me. I'm only wanting to help people with what I know, and now I'm being asked to hone in on people's deepest insecurities and wildest dreams to get them to read my book. What kind of person do you think I am?* I can see where you're coming from, but let's look at it from a different angle. If your aim is for your book to help people, those people have to want to read it. And for them to want to read it, it must call to them from the bookshelves. The only way it will do that is if it's solving a burning problem – the one thing that if they didn't have to deal with it would make their lives infinitely better.

When your readers have an obsessive fear or frustration that they want to remove, or an overwhelming desire or goal that they want to fulfil, they're in the market to buy a book about it. That book could be yours. What are your readers' fears, desires, goals, and frustrations? Grab a notebook or fire up a spreadsheet and list as many of them as you can. Then hone them down so that you have one or two to focus on.

Their age, gender, and lifestyle

If you're writing a book about retirement or parenting, for instance, it's pretty clear what life stage your readers are at. But it's also important to pin down their personal characteristics, even if your topic isn't age or gender specific.

This is where self-help authors can come unstuck. Suppose your book is about goal-setting – a topic that's surely relevant to readers of any gender, at any age, and of any lifestyle. Why narrow it down? Because if you don't, your content will be of generic appeal to fewer people than if you'd been targeted about it. Writing that's couched in general terms is hard work to absorb – readers must deduce for themselves how it applies to their lives rather than it being obvious. To see what I mean, think about the difference between these two sentences from an imaginary book that's about how to sleep well:

When you want to sleep soundly at night, it's important to eliminate stresses and distractions before bedtime.

When you want to sleep soundly at night, it's important to turn off your phone, switch off your laptop, and make it clear to your boss or clients that you're not available for emails after 7pm.

The first sentence is aimed at 'anyone' who finds it hard to destress before bedtime. The second is aimed at employees and business owners who work from home (or bring their work home with them) and have demanding jobs that are hard to get away from. It's obvious who the book is for, and to those overworked souls who will benefit from it, it's far more meaningful.

This points to another advantage of being specific about your readership, which is that your examples and stories will be more relevant. Let's take the example of goal-setting again. This is an activity that can take place in many different contexts: at work, in relationships, in finances, and in nutrition, to name but a few. Your selected readers will have one or two top of mind when they come across your book, and you want them to know that it's the right guide for them. If they're high-earning women aged 30–50 with successful careers and a family at home, they won't relate to stories that are grounded in landing a first job or saving enough for a deposit on a flat. Your book won't resonate with them. But if your examples are based on gaining their next promotion or helping their children to do well in exams, they'll see where you're coming from.

If narrowing your book's audience worries you, please take comfort in this. It's a weird fact that when we read a book that we see is aimed at a different audience to ourselves, we can still get a lot out of it. In fact, we relate to it more easily than if we're not sure who it's for in the first place. Your readers are no different. When you make it clear who your book is for right from the start, many of them will stick with it and be happy to 'translate' your advice into their own lives. They'll even find this simpler than if they're confused about whether it's for them. So please don't worry about being picky with who your readers are; it's an essential part of writing a good book.

Thinking of your own book, what kind of people are your readers? Consider the basic stuff such as gender, age, and job, but also wider lifestyle choices: what they like to do in their spare time, what kinds of relationships they have, and what sparks their enthusiasm. Take a moment to write them down, then reorder them from most to least important.

Aligning your topic with your readers

Picture a plait, or braid, in a girl's hair. It's impossible to tell which set of strands is which, because once they're interwoven they make up one harmonious whole. That's how your book's topic and its target readership should be. Your topic is for a particular set of readers, and those readers are obsessed with learning about your topic. One can't work without the other.

Here's a simple but powerful exercise that you can use to be clear on how your topic relates to your readers and vice versa. I confess that I didn't invent it myself, and I wish I could remember who I learned it from as I've found it incredibly helpful when planning my clients' books with them (whoever you are, thank you).

It consists of three statements for you to complete.

- *I'm sick and tired of* [enter your readers' key problem as they see it]
- *I wish I could* [enter the state or situation that your readers would love instead]
- *But I don't know* [enter the information that your readers are lacking, which if they had it would give them the transformation they desire]

Here are a couple of examples. '*I'm sick and tired of* seeing unfairness in the world. *I wish I could* help to create a more equal society, *but I don't know* how to talk to the right people in the right way so that I can set things in motion.' Or '*I'm sick and tired of* going on diets and putting the weight on afterwards. *I wish I could* keep it off for good. *But I don't know* how to generate the willpower to do that – it seems impossible.'

Note that neither of these people frames their problem in the way that you might as the author of the book they're about to read. In the first example, the reader wants to learn how to become an activist, but they probably wouldn't describe it that way if you asked them. Instead, they see their issues as being a lack of confidence and networking skills. The second reader wants to learn how to eat healthily and enjoyably for the rest of their life, but again they probably wouldn't talk about it like that. Instead, they perceive that developing more willpower is the way to reach their goal.

Completing these statements is an excellent way of stepping into your target reader's head and looking at the world through their eyes. It's only when you've done this that you can write for them in a way that they appreciate and understand. It also helps you to complete the process of deciding the core topic and readership of your book. You know who your readers are, what their main problem is, where they'd like to get to by solving it, and what they see as the barriers to doing so. You're now fully set for the final part of your book definition process, which is to decide what kind of self-help guide you're going to write.

The landmarks

- Your book must have a tightly defined target readership if it's to resonate with the right people.

- Ways of defining it include thinking about your readers' key problem as they see it; their desires, fears, goals, and frustrations; and their age, gender, and lifestyle.

- Your book's core topic should be closely interwoven with the nature of its readership.

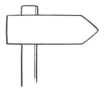

4. Your readers' journey

Your book will take its readers on a journey. What kind will it be? A road trip, a backpacker's expedition, a safari, a hill walk? Or something else? Each of these offers a different experience – a specific flavour of journey – and your task is to decide which one is most suited to your topic and audience. In other words, what kind of self-help guide you're writing.

There are many ways to present the information in your book, and you might already have decided what you want or you may not have given it much thought. Whichever it is, let's think about it from a strategic perspective, because if you don't have a framework for organizing your content you might select a format just because you like the look of it rather than because it will work for your readers. Or (just as possibly) you may not even realize that you're working with a format at all, and veer from one to another without knowing it. This could give your book an unfocused and disjointed feel which will make it disorientating to read.

When a self-help book isn't a self-help book

One of the things about personal self-help books that can set authors on the wrong track is that they can be mistaken for other types of books, and this makes planning the book more complicated than it needs to be. In my experience, there are four 'disguises' that a self-help book can take, which are based on not knowing the difference between:

- A self-help book and a memoir
- A self-help book and a thought-leadership book
- A self-help book and a how-to book
- A personal self-help book and a business self-help book

Please be aware that these terms aren't just labels; they dictate the structure, tone, and content of your book in a fundamental way. The good news is that, once you understand the key differences between these kinds of books, you'll be in a position to select the one that works for you. I'll take each in turn.

Self-help book OR memoir?

If your primary aim is to help people to achieve a personal transformation in their lives, it's a self-help guide you're writing, not a memoir. In a self-help book, you take your readers on a journey from problem to solution by sharing your expertise. Your personal story will be included, but it won't be the focus of the book. An example of this is Gretchen Rubin's *The Happiness Project*. It talks about how to create a happier life, and while the author makes plentiful use of her own experiences throughout, it's secondary to the teaching points within it.

However, if your primary aim is to entertain and inspire your readers by recounting your personal story, it's a memoir, not a self-help book. In a memoir, you tell the story that led to your personal transformation and, unlike in a self-help book, you don't make explicit teaching points.

There's also a difference in your readers' expectations when you compare the two types of book. In a self-help guide, your readers expect to learn specific things that they can apply to their lives. In a memoir, on the other hand, your readers expect to be moved and entertained, as Elizabeth Gilbert achieves in *Eat, Pray, Love*. It's a story about the author's travels abroad and her resulting journey of personal growth, but she doesn't make any overt points about what her readers should learn. It's up to them whether they want to make changes to their own lives after reading it.

'But I aim to do both,' you say. 'I've had life experiences that have been transformational for me and that have led to the client work I carry out today. I want my readers to learn from my expertise, but I also need to talk about my story so that they can see where I'm coming from.'

That makes a lot of sense, but you need to decide which is most important. If you try to do both equally, you won't be successful with either. Readers won't know what to expect from your book (which is the kiss of death for your sales) and bookstores won't know what shelf to put it on: memoir or self-help. Even more importantly, it won't be clear to those who do read it what they're supposed to get out of it. Are they meant to learn from your teaching points or from your story? In other words, do they expect to be taught or to teach themselves?

If you decide that you want primarily to inspire your readers through your story, and that it's therefore a memoir you're writing, that's fine. This book isn't the one that will help you to do that, but at least you know before you've spent time writing something that sits between two stools. On the other hand, if you decide that you want to teach your readers explicitly and that it's therefore a self-help guide you're writing, you're in the right place. Of course, your book can still contain lots of stories and examples from your personal experiences – the more the merrier. But these will be incidental to the lessons and how-tos that make up the 'meat' of your book. We'll explore this balance later, but if you'd like to read a book that combines the two excellently, *Option B* by Sheryl Sandberg and Adam Grant is a sound choice, as is *The Long Win* by Cath Bishop.

To summarize: do you want your readers to learn specific lessons and put them into practice in their lives? If so, you're writing a self-help book. Or do you want to entertain and inspire your readers with your personal story? If so, you're writing a memoir.

Self-help book OR thought-leadership book?

Some authors come to their books with a burning desire to educate the world about their area of expertise; they want to change things, make waves, and transform society for the better. They've usually become knowledgeable about their subject through personal experience, professional training and study, or both.

The result is what's often called a thought-leadership book. These books are excellent vehicles for putting across complex and controversial arguments and, if they're successful, for establishing their authors as major players on the world stage. They can also stand the test of time; people are still reading Germaine Greer's *The Female Eunuch* and Machiavelli's *The Prince* today. More contemporary examples are *Quiet* by Susan Cain, which extols the power of introversion and calls for a new attitude towards quiet, sensitive people; and Lynne Twist's *The Soul of Money*, which explores how examining our attitudes towards money can give us transformational insights into our lives and make the world a better place.

So, what's the difference between a thought-leadership and a self-help book? Interestingly, their aims are the same: to create an inner change in the reader that will hopefully be reflected in outer action. However, a self-help guide makes overt teaching points, whereas a thought-leadership book doesn't. Instead, a thought-leadership book uses a combination of storytelling and theoretical exposition to put across the author's points.

If you're finding it hard to know which type to write, ask yourself this: 'Do I want my readers to think differently about something, or do I want them to think differently about something *and* learn specific lessons that they can apply to their lives?' If it's the former it's a thought-leadership book, and if it's the latter it's a self-help guide.

Self-help book OR how-to book?

If I'm honest, it's a bit disingenuous to pretend that there's a distinction between how-to and self-help, because all self-help includes a strong element of how-to. Suppose you were writing a book about giving up alcohol; you'd want to include some how-to information, such as:

- Tips for cutting out the booze
- Ways of maintaining sobriety
- How to build a support network

If you didn't have those how-to elements, your book would be theoretical rather than grounded in practical advice – and that would be of limited help to your readers.

So any self-help guide will contain some how-tos, but the difference between a how-to and a self-help book lies in the intention behind it. The 'going sober' book is a self-help guide because it creates a transformation in its readers from alcohol dependency to sobriety, with the how-tos as an aid to achieving this. However, a guide to DIY in the home, which has the intention of instructing its readers in the art of shelf-fixing and wallpaper-pasting, isn't concerned with personal transformation and is therefore a how-to book. Of course, its readers may grow in confidence as they tackle jobs around the house for the first time, but that's not primarily what the book is designed to achieve.

Personal self-help book OR business self-help book?

This is an easy area to get mixed up about. There are many books that help people to succeed in business, whether it be by teaching them about marketing, managing teams, or any number of things that it's important for a businessperson to do well. Some of these books are aimed at business owners and some at people in certain professions, but either way they're designed to help their readers achieve specific outcomes at work. An example is *Brand Storytelling* by Miri Rodriguez, which explains why people should place stories at the heart of their business marketing. By the end of the book, they should understand the principles behind storytelling and how to put them into practice.

So, business self-help guides do offer a transformation, but it's not a personal one. There's a level of crossover, because becoming a more effective HR manager, for instance, might make you feel better about yourself. But they're not personal self-help books in that their focus is on the work skill and not on the inner person.

You might feel that your book enables people to do both: perform more highly at work *and* in their personal lives. This could be the case if your topic is based on thinking and behaviour that takes place in both work and life, such as communication skills, confidence, and decision-making. But it's still better if you choose which context is most important, because it affects how you present your information. If you're writing a business self-help book your stories and examples will be work-based, whereas if it's a personal self-help book they'll take inspiration from family life, friendships, and private activities. When your readers are immersed in either one world or the other, they'll find it easier to translate theory into practice.

The different formats

Here's where it gets exciting. As part of my research for writing this book, I went through the numerous personal development guides on my bookshelf and Kindle, plus those that I'd been recommended by others. I wanted to see what approaches their authors took to the way they outlined them. What formats did they use?

What I didn't realize until I did this was *how many ways* there are to structure a self-help book – it's a highly flexible genre. The formats below are by no means all there is. You might want to go through a similar exercise with the books you own or think about a personal development guide that you found inspiring and useful, and ask yourself what it was about it that made it work for you. You may find clues in it about how to structure your own book.

Here are the main formats that I've come across, together with examples, reasons why you might want to use them, and potential pitfalls to watch out for.

Step by step

The steps in a self-help guide can be organized in various ways: chronologically (Day One, Day Two) or some other sequential way ('First do this, then do that').

Examples: *The Big Leap* by Gay Hendricks, in which the author takes his readers on a four-step process that will enable them to solve their 'upper-limit' problem. Also *The Artist's Way* by Julia Cameron, which gives its readers different exercises to do each week for 12 weeks, with the aim of unlocking their creativity.

Why you might want to use it: it's clear and makes it easy to for readers to put your teachings into action. That's why the step-by-step format is one of the most popular for self-help guides.

What to watch out for: it only works if your topic can be broken down into time-bound or sequential steps.

Grouped by theme

This is when a book covers different aspects of a topic in a thematic rather than a sequential way. You can think of each aspect as being like a spoke on a wheel, with the spokes pointing to the same core problem.

Examples: *Playing Big* by Tara Mohr, which goes through the key thought patterns that hold women back, each in a different chapter. Also *The Sober Survival Guide* by Simon Chapple, in which the author examines a separate challenge to giving up alcohol, chapter by chapter.

Why you might want to use it: it's a clear, comprehensive, and flexible structure for you as an author. It also means that, to a certain extent, you can arrange your chapters in whatever order you like.

What to watch out for: it only works if the destination you want your readers to reach doesn't depend on learning one thing before the next. It might be that there are some 'basic' topics that are best covered before the 'advanced' ones, but overall the order shouldn't be the most important thing.

Based on your programme

If you already have a successful training programme that you use with your clients, you can base the structure of your book on that.

Example: *Creating the Impossible* by Michael Neill. In this, the author replicates his popular online programme which encourages people to achieve things that they never thought were within their power. The 'real-life' programme is 90 days long and the book, after some initial introductory chapters, is based on a chapter a day for the same period of time.

Why you might want to use it: if you already have a programme that works well, it avoids reinventing the wheel. Also, if you want to use your book as a way of bringing people into your programme, it's helpful for them if they have a similar experience across the two. This is also the case for readers who've taken part in your programme and want to use your book as a way of supplementing what they've learned.

What to watch out for: don't assume that it's simply a matter of taking your course content and putting it into a book. Your readers don't have the benefit of being in the room (or on screen) with you, so they need a different set of explanations than they do in person. And remember that they can't ask questions, so you'll need to deal with any potential objections and misunderstandings within your writing.

Many short chapters

Most self-help books are structured around 8 to 12 chapters, each based on a different element of the topic. However, it's possible to have a much larger number of shorter chapters, which gives your reader a different experience.

Examples: *Struggle* by Grace Marshall, which examines a different aspect of struggling in life within bite-sized chapters. The author structured it like this to make it easy for people who were finding life challenging to access advice and encouragement. Also *Real* by Clare Dimond, which explores a profound spiritual topic in an accessible way by using short chapters.

Why you might want to use this: if your readers are in the kind of situation that limits their attention span, for instance because of stress, mental health issues, or substance abuse, this is a digestible format for them. It also gives you the opportunity to make a complicated topic straightforward and unthreatening by breaking it down into multiple constituent parts.

What to watch out for: it can feel disjointed and bitty if you don't take care to organize the chapters in a logical way.

Made-up concept

This is when the author bases their teaching on a made-up analogy or concept, using it as a platform for putting across their points.

Examples: *Your Brain at Work* by David Rock, which employs the analogy of a director, actors, and a stage to teach its readers how to focus effectively at work. Also *The Chimp Paradox* by Professor Steve Peters, which uses the model of a chimp and seven planets to explain how our minds operate and how we can become happier and more content. (Fun fact: *The Chimp Paradox* is the biggest seller in Nielsen's UK self-improvement category since records began in 1998.)

Why you might want to use it: it's a superb way of making the abstract and complicated concrete and simple. When a theoretical idea is brought to life by a visual concept, it's easy for readers to grasp and remember what the author is teaching them.

What to watch out for: you need to make sure that your made-up concept is both solid and flexible enough to support your core idea. Also, be wary of stretching the concept too far; if it only works for the first section of the book, for instance, just use it there.

Series of exercises

This type of guide is usually made up of a set of activities for the reader to do. The idea is that the learning comes from actively participating in the exercises, rather than by reading the advice alone.

Examples: *The Artist's Way* by Julia Cameron, which takes its readers on a 12-week journey to reconnect with their creativity, with a different set of tasks to complete each week. Also *How to Talk So Kids Will Listen and Listen So Kids Will Talk* by Adele Faber and Elaine Mazlish, which makes liberal use of 'fill in the blanks' exercises.

Why you might want to use it: there's no better way to learn (and remember) something new than actively to try it out, and this format provides a safe space for readers to do that.

What to watch out for: for the exercises to work, you need to be able to transpose yourself into your readers' learning process; this takes some skill and experience. You also have to make the exercises highly engaging.

Question and answer

In this, the author bases their book on a series of questions that their readers might ask if they were with them face to face, and provides the answers.

Examples: *The Power of Now* by Eckhart Tolle; after a short introduction to the concept of 'the Now', the rest of the book is made up of questions that the author is most often asked, and his answers to them. Also, *Families and How to Survive Them* by Robin Skynner and John Cleese, which is more of a Socratic dialogue than a Q&A but is based on the same concept. In this, Skynner is the family therapist who answers Cleese's questions about how to create a happy family.

Why you might want to use it: this format works well if the basic lesson that you're imparting is relatively simple, but the implications take a lot of working through. It also reassures people that they're not alone with their questions, which helps them to feel secure enough to learn.

What to watch out for: it can't be a random collection of questions and answers – you still need to structure them in a way that takes your readers on a journey.

Two voices

This format uses two authors, each with a distinctive take on their subject. It could be that one has the story and the other the technical expertise to make sense of it, or it might be that both are experts but have different perspectives.

Example: *Will It Make the Boat Go Faster?* by Ben Hunt-Davis and Harriet Beveridge, which alternates between chapters by Olympic rower Hunt-Davis and performance coach Beveridge. Hunt-Davis tells the rollercoaster story of how he and his team won a gold medal, while Beveridge imparts teaching points about how we can improve our own performance in life.

Why you might want to use this: it's an interesting way of combining a transformational story with overt lessons, especially if you want to team up with an author who has expertise complementary to your own.

What to watch out for: it can feel disjointed for your readers unless sensitively handled, which is probably why this format isn't used as much as it could be.

Based on someone else's story
This format takes a narrative that already exists and extrapolates teaching points from it.

Examples: *The Tao of Pooh* by Benjamin Hoff, which explains the ancient principle of Taoism by comparing it to the stories of *Winnie the Pooh*. Also *Be More Pirate* by Sam Conniff Allende, which explores what we can learn from the golden age of pirates to help us achieve more in life.

Why you might want to use this: it provides an interesting and memorable foundation to your teaching points.

What to watch out for: you must be sure of your premise if you're to convince your readers of the parallels.

Organizing story
This format is based on a story that the author uses to organize their teaching points in an entertaining and digestible way.

Example: *The Wealthy Barber* by David Chilton, which tells the tale of a fictional barber who helps someone to manage their money more effectively. Through this, the book educates its readers in the art and science of creating financial independence.

Why you might want to use it: it's excellent for subjects that might otherwise seem 'boring', such as financial planning.

What to watch out for: it's not easy to tell an engaging story that works both as entertainment and teaching aide. You need top-notch storytelling skills.

Overall, most self-help guides fall into either the 'step-by-step' or 'grouped by theme' categories, and for good reason; they're simple and easy to structure, and it's hard to go wrong with them. But it's also good to think more widely about how you could present your material; maybe there's a format that grabs you and could give you the impetus to write your book.

Which will you choose? If you're finding it hard to decide, it's worth remembering that your book's structure must support all of the following:

- What you want to achieve with your book
- What it's about
- Who it's for (your readers)

A self-help book takes its readers on a journey of transformation, so that by the end they've experienced an internal shift. Ask yourself whether the format you've chosen will do that in the best way for your particular subject, for your specific readers, and given the aims you have in mind for both you and your book. Now, you're ready to start outlining your book.

The landmarks

- Your book's format dictates how you organize and present the material within it, and therefore how your readers will learn from it.
- It's important to be clear on the differences between self-help books and memoirs, thought-leadership books, how-to books, and business self-help books.

- There are many formats you can choose to work with, each with their own pros and cons.
- Which format you choose should be based on your personal preferences, your aims, your topic, and your readers.

OUTLINE YOUR BOOK: PLAN YOUR JOURNEY

5. Your road map

Now that you know what kind of self-help book you're writing, it's time to create an outline for it. This is important because, as I've probably hammered home too many times by now, it will be taking your readers on a journey. If you aren't crystal clear on what the start and end points are, and where the overnight stops will be along the way, you'll be in danger of getting lost. When that happens, your readers won't receive the benefit you want them to have – the transformation that you're offering.

I've divided the process of outlining into two short chapters: your road map and your detailed itinerary. This one focuses on the road map, which is the big-picture plan describing your destination and the locations you'll stay in along the way. It's the broad trajectory of your book.

How to create your big-picture plan

I work with many authors who feel overwhelmed by the thoughts and ideas swimming around in their heads; they're not sure what to start with, or which bits of information to leave in and take out. Maybe you're in the same boat. If you don't find creating a top-line structure to be easy or intuitive process, here's a simple three-step way of approaching it.

1. Decide your format
2. Pinpoint your readers' starting place and end destination
3. Plot your way points

1. Decide your format
This is what we covered in the previous chapter. Decide what type of journey you're leading your readers on, remembering to take into account what you want to achieve with your book, who your readers are, and what your book is about (its 'gold').

2. Pinpoint your readers' starting place and destination
In Chapter 1 we looked at the change you're leading your readers through, and in Chapters 2 and 3 we explored how your topic relates to what those readers want. Now is when you stick a pin in the map to mark the exact place that you're 'meeting' your readers at the beginning of your book.

Let me explain what I mean. Imagine that you're excited about going on holiday – it's going to be a super-relaxing, poolside break interspersed with trips to restaurants and, if you're feeling energetic enough, to the beach. But how far along are you on the journey that you're about to take? Are you packing your bags? At the airport checking in? Or on the plane saying, 'Yes I'll have a gin and tonic please'? In the same way, where are your readers 'at' with their transition when they open the first page of your book? Are they at the departure gate or are they still stuffing clothes into suitcases? Could they even be at the end of week one? If you don't know where they are, you won't be able to talk to them in a way that's meaningful for them, and you risk losing their interest from the word go.

Suppose you want to help people in their 50s to move from being stuck in their career to feeling fulfilled. What's the conversation that these people are having with themselves about their problem before they pick up your book? It could be any of the following and more:

- Surely there's more to life than this dead-end job?
- Managers will never give someone my age a chance.
- I'm too old to learn new skills.

Each of these examples points to a different starting place for your readers. The first is the dissatisfied feeling that prompts them to seek help with changing their career. The second is the assumption that other people are getting in their way. And the third is that they're not capable of change. Whatever their starting place, this is where you must join them. If they're telling themselves that they're too old to learn new skills, for instance, there would be little point in you beginning with an exhortation to go on training courses – they'd brush aside your advice as being irrelevant and wonder why they'd bought your book. Instead, you'd need to spend some time persuading them that they're capable of personal growth and that it's easier than they think; *then* you can go into the mechanics of how they could go about it.

This is where many self-help authors go wrong – they start from the place that they think their readers *should* be at, or where they *assume* they're at, rather than where they're *actually* at. And they lose credibility because they come across as not understanding their readers, who are likely to turn to a different book – one that speaks more directly to their needs.

So that's your readers' starting place, but what about their destination? This is easier. You identified that in Chapter 1, so why not revisit it now? It's important to be clear on what it is because you're about to work out how you're going to get them there.

3. Plot your way points

If you know the format that you want to use, your starting place, and your destination, this part of the process is simply a matter of deciding what points to make and what order to put them in. The result will be your table of contents.

First, let's look at how you decide what main points to make. I suggest that you use one of two methods for this: mind-mapping or sticky notes. Which one you choose depends on whether or not you're a visual person; if you are, I suggest the mind map route, and if not, the sticky notes. Either way, your next step is to ask yourself this question: What, given the big problem your readers have, is the first thing they need to do to solve it? Write it down on your mind map or sticky note and put it on your wall.

Now ask yourself what other things they need to think about and do, and do the same. Don't worry about whether they're in the right order for your book, just put them down. Let your mind have free rein. By the end of this process, you'll have a mind map that probably looks pretty disorganized or a forest of sticky notes, each with a single point on.

Then, when you've written down everything you can think of that relates to how you'll take your readers from starting point to destination, take a step back. Maybe even have a cup of tea – you've earned it. Ask yourself how you could group your points, given the format that you've chosen. If you're creating a mind map you can draw lines between them, and if your wall is festooned with sticky notes you can reposition them into neat columns, each labelled with a separate topic at the top.

For instance, if yours is a themed guide to developing a more intimate relationship with your partner, your groups might be labelled thus:

1. Introduction
2. The benefits of improving your relationship
3. What does intimacy mean to you?
4. Common relationship problems
5. How to stop arguing
6. Ways of communicating more effectively
7. The importance of spending quality time together
8. Ways to improve your sex life
9. Conclusion

I'm making this up, of course – I'm not a relationships expert and can only guess at what I'd write about if I were. But you can see how I've grouped all my points into eight top-level chapter themes that make sense. In this case it's a themed format so it doesn't matter too much which chapter comes first, second, or third, but it does work well having chapters 2, 3, and 4 early on as they set my readers up with some background information before I dive into how to change their relationships.

You can also divide your book into parts, each with its own set of chapters. This helps to organize your content so that the major steps are obvious to your readers. An example of a book that does this well is *Atomic Habits* by James Clear. He starts with a part called 'The Fundamentals', which contains three chapters detailing why tiny changes make a difference. Then he has four further parts entitled 'The 1st Law', 'The 2nd Law', and so on, each containing three or four chapters. Finally, he has a part called 'Advanced Tactics', which gives readers ways of taking further action if they want to. All book-ended with an Introduction and Conclusion.

After you've created your table of contents, take a moment to think about whether there's anything important missing. You're an expert in your subject but your readers are not. Putting yourself in their shoes, are there any significant gaps in your road map? Could people get lost along the way? To help you, think of the questions that your clients normally ask when they work with you; would they be answered by the content of your chapter headings?

On the other hand, your book isn't the place to put everything you know. Consider your tightly defined readership – what do they need to learn in order to solve the one pressing problem that's brought them to your book? They don't want to feel overwhelmed or confused by too much information, they just want to be taken by the hand and led on the journey that will get them to the right place. It can be hard to appreciate how little someone needs to know to make a significant change in their lives; just because you have more insights than that, doesn't mean you should include them all.

There's also another reason for being conservative about what you include, which is that you might be tempted to incorporate topics you're not completely sure about. Think of your expertise as having three levels.

Core knowledge
Competent knowledge
Second-hand knowledge

The three levels of expertise

The top level is your core knowledge – the stuff that you're rock solid on, have unique experience of, and enjoy helping people with the most. The middle level is what you're competent enough to advise people on, but it's not the reason for what you do. And the bottom level is what you're less sure of; you might have read books about it or been on a course, but you've not practised it in person. It's best not to clutter your book with the bottom level and to be limited in what you include from the middle. Instead, create a book that's bursting with value by focusing on your top tier of knowledge, trusting that other people have written great books on the rest.

To give you an example, as a ghostwriter and book coach my top level is strategizing and writing non-fiction books. My middle level is publishing and marketing books, and my lower level is the technicalities of self-publishing and also of public speaking to promote books. So when I wrote my guide to planning, writing, and promoting a business book, *Your Business Your Book,* I left out the bottom level and was limited in what I included from the middle one. There was more than enough to talk about from the top, and my book did a better job as a result. (Being honest, it was also a massive relief when I realized that I didn't have to write about the stuff that I wasn't so confident about.)

How do you know when you've created a table of contents that works? I'll leave this to the eloquent words of publishing expert Alison Jones:

> Your table of contents is a map of the book. You know the territory already so it might not seem that important to you, but to your readers it is everything. They'll look at the table of contents and ask themselves, 'Does this look like a place I want to go? Does it look like it's going to be a fun journey? And do I trust this author to take me there? Is it clear? Is it signposted? Is it thought through?' If it's just a long list of vague, unrelated headings, how are they going to trust you as a guide?[3]

Now that you have your table of contents mapped out, congratulations! It's starting to look like a real book. Next, we'll look at what to say in each chapter.

The landmarks

- Outlining before you write makes your book better and easier to complete than if you skip it.
- It's important to know where you're 'meeting' your readers at the beginning of your book.
- Your table of contents provides the framework for your book and needs to show your readers the journey that they're about to embark on.

---

[3] http://extraordinarybusinessbooks.com/episode-304-things-that-editors-love

6. Your detailed itinerary

Here's what, in my experience, most people do when they write their first chapter. They look at their road map or table of contents and think, *So this chapter is about laying the foundations for becoming more resilient. What's the first thing I want to say about that?* Then they write it down. After that they think, *What's the next thing I could say about it?* Then they write that down. And so on, until all the thoughts that they have about the subject are down on the page.

The result of this is a chapter that makes a lot of sense to them but doesn't necessarily take their readers on the voyage of discovery that will change their lives. That's because when you write your points as they occur to you, you're not structuring them in a way that works for someone who's new to the topic. You may also find that when you review your writing a few days later, something seems a bit off about it and it's hard to work out what it is or how to fix it. Fear not – the chapter you're reading now is where you'll learn two golden techniques for organizing what you want to say.

Two ways to plot your points

Go back to your mind map or forest of sticky notes and take another look at the points you've noted for each chapter. As yet they're not in any logical order, only how they came to mind when you wrote them down. What should go first, second, third, and so on? How do you decide? There are two processes that you can use.

Why? What? How? What if?

This isn't my own framework but is one that many trainers use. Its basis is that we each have our own bias when it comes to learning about something new. Some of us need to know *why* we should learn something before we can feel motivated enough to read about it. Some of us want to know *what* is important about a topic – the explanation of the significant facts. Some of us want to know *how* to do something and feel frustrated if this isn't explained. And others of us think that it's vital to know the *what if?* – the real-world consequences of taking the advice.

- Why?
- What?
- How?
- What if?

Which is your bias when you learn something new? Mine is *why* – I have to know this before I move forward with the *what*, otherwise I can't see the point. On the other hand, I'm rarely interested in *how*; this means that, if I'm not careful, I can gloss over the 'how to' when I write advice for other people because

I'm assuming that it's not important to them either. This is why it's incredibly helpful to understand your own bias.

The other reason that this technique is useful is because it gets you away from writing your points in the order that they occur to you. Instead, you're thinking about them in the order that will be most persuasive for your readers, which is infinitely more effective.

Let's look at an example. Suppose I'm writing a book for people who want to simplify their lives, and one of my chapters is on the topic of decluttering their homes. If I was to order my points in the chapter according to the method above, my plan might look something like this:

Why declutter?

- Makes you feel calmer
- Enables you to find what you need
- Helps you to appreciate what you have
- Your home looks more attractive

What decluttering is

- A process of thinking about what's important in your life
- A way of identifying what you do and don't need, and getting rid of the latter

How to declutter

- Set aside enough time and have bin bags or a skip handy.
- Do it room by room.

- Pick one area and go through it piece by piece, asking yourself whether what you're holding is important enough to keep.

- If you're not sure, ask yourself when the last time was that you used an item; if it was over two years ago, throw it out.

- When you have a full bag, take it out and start on another one.

- Reward yourself when the room is done.

What if the decluttering doesn't go well?

- Be kind to yourself – at least you've made a start.

- Take a break and come back to it.

- Switch to an easier space or room.

- If there are things that you need to get rid of but find it hard to be parted from, take photos of them and then throw them out.

What if the decluttering does go well?

- Bask in the glory of your newly ordered home.

- Invite friends round without feeling embarrassed by the mess.

You'll see that I've kept my points as bullets. This is helpful for you too, because it gives you the opportunity to reorganize them before you start writing actual paragraphs (yes, you're about to do that). When all that you have is a list in front of you, it's simple to spot when something is in the wrong order, is missing, or shouldn't be there in the first place. As soon as you're looking at paragraphs, it becomes much harder to work out whether the flow of points makes sense.

One final thing: some authors can find it hard to distinguish between points that should be in the *What* section and those that should be in the *How*. Here's another way of telling the difference. Ask yourself what kind of language you'll be using for each: *What* is a description, whereas *How* is effectively a set of instructions. If you use the analogy of a recipe, *What* is the description of the dish and the list of ingredients, and *How* is the directions for combining them.

Chunking

The above method works for the most popular self-help book formats, but there's another that you can use as well. I call it 'chunking', and it derives from a technique that I learned from ghostwriter Claudia Suzanne. This is especially useful when you've already written a chapter and, when reviewing it, decide that it's what can only be described as a 'hot mess' — it has everything in it, but is about as organized as a plate of spaghetti. You don't want to delete it and start again but are lost as to how to fix it (we've all been there). It's also helpful if you're working with a format that doesn't lend itself well to the Why, What, How, and What If? structure.

Step 1: For chunking you need two things: your chapter and a spreadsheet (or a table in a Word document). Your spreadsheet or table will have three columns, headed from left to right: 'Sequence', 'Revised sequence', and 'Topic'.

Sequence	Revised sequence	Topic

Chunking step 1

Step 2: Enter numbers 1 to 6 in the first six rows of the 'Sequence' column on the left of the spreadsheet, like this:

Sequence	Revised sequence	Topic
1		
2		
3		
4		
5		
6		

Chunking step 2

Step 3: Read the first paragraph of your 'hot mess' chapter. Ask yourself: given the purpose of this chapter, what overall point is this a part of? And how would I summarize that overall point in five to ten words? For instance, if the paragraph is about possessions that you've had for so long that they've become part of the furniture, the overall point might be 'How to decide if something is worth keeping'. Write 'How to decide if something is worth keeping' on row 1 on your spreadsheet.

Step 4. Enter the number 1 in a different colour at the end of the paragraph, so it's easy to see. This paragraph is now assigned to that section.

Sequence	Revised sequence	Topic
1		How to decide if something is worth keeping
2		
3		
4		
5		
6		

Chunking steps 3 and 4

Step 5: Do the same for each of the paragraphs in your chapter. You'll find that multiple paragraphs can be assigned the same number.

Step 6: Add in extra numbers if you need to but try not to go above 10–15 points or your chapter may become unwieldy.

Your spreadsheet could end up looking something like this.

Sequence	Revised sequence	Topic
1	5	How to decide if something is worth keeping
2	1	Why declutter?
3	2	Pratical preparations for decluttering
4	6	Another topic...
5	3	Another topic...
6	4	Another topic...

Chunking steps 5 and 6

Step 7: Now take a break and revisit your numbered list of points on the spreadsheet. Knowing your readers as you do, what order do you think that they should go in? Try not to overthink this – you already have the answer in your head and are just using this process to help you access it.

Step 8: Enter the revised order numbers in the 'Revised sequence' column. You now have two columns, each with the same numbers but in a different order.

Sequence	Revised sequence	Topic
1	5	How to decide if something is worth keeping
2	1	Why declutter?
3	2	Pratical preparations for decluttering
4	6	Another topic...
5	3	Another topic...
6	4	Another topic...

Chunking steps 7 and 8

Step 9: If you're using a spreadsheet, highlight the whole sheet and sort your columns by 'Revised sequence', smallest to largest. If you're using a Word document, you'll need to do this manually.

Step 10: You now have a 'Revised sequence' column that shows the new order of your points, alongside the original number and description of each. In other words, you've rejigged your entire chapter.

Sequence	Revised sequence	Topic
2	1	Why declutter?
3	2	Pratical preparations for decluttering
5	3	Another topic...
6	4	Another topic...
1	5	How to decide if something is worth keeping
4	6	Another topic...

Chunking step 10

Step 11: Go through your chapter, cutting and pasting the paragraphs into the new 'Revised sequence' order. You'll need to rewrite it so that it makes sense and flows, but this is far quicker than starting again from scratch or trying to work it out as you go along.

Honestly, reading this process is twice as hard as actually doing it; by the time you've used it for a couple of chapters, you'll see how quickly you can put your points in order. It takes the angst out of things by encouraging you to view your content objectively as a set of summaries, rather than being overwhelmed by too much detail.

Now that you've planned and plotted your points to perfection, you're ready to fire up your creativity. It's time to become a compelling and persuasive writer.

The landmarks

- The order that your points go in is important; they need to lead your readers on a journey of discovery.

- Use *Why? What? How? What if?* to make sure that you're describing things in an order that makes sense for them.

- Alternatively (or as well), use chunking to organize your content.

WRITE YOUR BOOK: EMBARK ON YOUR JOURNEY

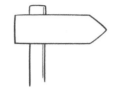

7. Be clear

By their very nature, self-help topics can be abstract: discover your purpose; heal your relationship; learn to communicate with your kids. And, like all such concepts, they can be hard for your readers to visualize and get their heads around. That's why clear writing is at the core of any successful personal development book. In their guide *Book Builder*, Lucy McCarraher and Joe Gregory call this being 'kind to your readers'.[4] They go on to say that 'if there's a hard way or an easy way to say something, use the easy way. If there's a long way or a short way to describe something, take the short route.' I can't think of a better way of putting it. After all, if your readers don't understand what you're telling them, they won't be able to make the changes that will get them to their destination. Make that journey as easy for them as possible.

---

[4] L. MacCarraher and J. Gregory, *Bookbuilder: the definitive guide to writing the book to transform your business* (2020), 91.

How do you give your book the clarity it needs? There are three keys to this:

- The way you organize it
- The way you word it
- What you put with it

The way you organize it

You already have a table of contents and an ordered list of points for each chapter, so you're well on the way to having a clear way of structuring your writing. However, there are some other approaches you can take to make your book an easy read.

Introductions

Each chapter needs an introduction so that your readers not only know what to expect from it but also why they should read it. Yes, really – they do need to feel motivated to take the time to read each and every chapter of your book. You can't take this for granted.

There are many ways to introduce a chapter:

- Explain what it will be about – this encourages your readers to relax, so they feel confident about what's to come.

- Tell your readers what they'll learn from it – this prepares them to take in new knowledge and motivates them to read on.

- Start with a story, a surprising fact or a quotation – this piques their interest.

- Ask them a question that's relevant to what they're about to learn – this gets them thinking.

- Empathize with your readers about whatever issue the chapter is designed to tackle – this encourages them to relax and trust you, because they know that you understand their issues.

You can also use these techniques when beginning a new section within a chapter; it's just as important for your readers to be kept on track while they're going through it as it is at the start. For instance, if you're writing a weight-loss guide and your chapter is about aids to weight loss, you might cover the topics of both supplements and meal replacement products. When transitioning from one to the other, you need to introduce them individually. If you don't, your train of thought won't be clear to your readers, and they'll find it hard to put what you're about to explain into a context that they can understand.

Summaries

I'm sure that you've read many personal development guides (including this one) that summarize the key learning points at the end of each chapter, and the reason this is such a popular technique is because it works. It's the adage: 'Tell 'em what you're going to tell 'em. Tell 'em. Then tell 'em what you've told 'em.' We learn best when we read things more than once, so it's helpful if you reiterate what you've just said.

Often a summary works best as a list of bullet points because lists are easy to digest and remember. But your chapter conclusion doesn't have to work that way – you can give a narrative summary instead. Just make sure that whatever method you use is concise and light on detail, and that you don't introduce any new material at this stage. You're only wanting to reinforce what you've already explained.

Subheadings

It's hard work reading a whole chapter of unbroken text, which is why subheadings help to make your writing easy to read. They fulfil a dual purpose: breaking up the chapter so that it's more digestible and signposting the topic to come.

Try to give your subheadings some thought. Most authors treat them as labels for what's to follow ('How herbal remedies help with stress'), and given that clarity is important, there's nothing wrong with that. However, you can also use your subheadings as a way of drawing your readers onwards, by giving them a twist. Ways of doing this include using surprise to grab their attention ('What's really going on when you feel stressed'); intrigue to pique their curiosity ('The way to beat stress that makes no sense at first'); and emotion ('Easy relief from stress').

The way you word it

This is about how you write with clarity, and is both the hardest and easiest thing you'll do when writing your book. It's hard because being clear involves having a deep insight into how your readers are thinking and feeling. And yet it's easy because you only have to make one leap – you to them – to make yourself understood. Once you've done that, everything you write stands a high chance of bringing your readers on board.

Your standpoint

Imagine that you're playing a game of charades. You have the title you want people to guess (let's say it's *Gone with the Wind*), and you're throwing yourself into it with gusto. Four words… first word… sounds like… aargh, you can't think of anything that rhymes with 'gone'. Never mind, let's move to the fourth word: 'wind'. You run around the room puffing out your cheeks and waving your arms, but all anyone can do is throw out guesses like 'dancer' or 'mad person'. Why can't they see it's the wind you're enacting? Surely it's obvious? What's *wrong* with them?

Which is, of course, where the fun comes in. But the interaction between you and your audience in this parlour game has a serious point to make, which is that while you're frantically acting out the title of a blockbuster book and film, you have knowledge of the information you're trying to put across. Your audience, however, isn't privy to this and has only your virtuoso performance to go on. What you imagine to be a set of meaningful gestures is, to them, a bizarre and unfathomable display.

This is why, when you write a self-help guide, you need to mentally regress yourself until you're at the same place as your readers. How far along the road are they in terms of their knowledge and expertise? What do they already know about the subject that you're teaching them? In my experience, it's usually a lot less than you think. Remember back to when you first came across your field of expertise. What assumptions did you have? What was confusing for you? Where did you stumble the most? Then move yourself along until you've reached the place where your readers are at now. It might be at the beginning of your journey or it might be further along, but whichever it is, you'll now be positioned to speak to them in a way that they'll understand.

Your language

It goes without saying that using professional jargon and terminology is a bad idea when you're wanting to be clear in your writing. But there's another aspect to your language that also merits consideration, which is being concrete rather than abstract.

A fun and effective way to do this is to use analogies as a way of explaining your concepts. For instance, if you're writing a book for women who want to increase their self-confidence, you could liken the experience of standing up to someone for the first time to going out for the evening without makeup. You feel vulnerable and naked at first, but after a while it feels good to be yourself.

Another way to make the abstract concrete is to use metaphors and similes.[5] These do the 'heavy lifting' for your ideas by using images to represent them (see what I did there?). In her book about anxiety, *A Little Peace of Mind*, Nicola Bird asks her readers to imagine that they're about to take a course in 'Snargleblart'.[6] This is her way of introducing the notion that what they'll learn will be totally foreign to them because it's such a new take on what they already think about their problem. Another example is in *Big Magic*, Elizabeth Gilbert's book about embracing your creativity.[7] She talks about ideas as being living entities that float around until they find someone who will welcome them and put them to use; if they don't find a home in us (the reader), they'll keep visiting new people until they have success.

One of my favourite books on analogies is *I Never Metaphor I Didn't Like* by Dr Mardy Grothe.[8] In it he gives countless examples of metaphors that have been used throughout the

---

[5] A metaphor is a direct comparison that states one thing is another; for instance, 'a blanket of snow'. A simile is an indirect comparison that uses 'as' or 'like'; for instance, 'the snow was like a blanket'.

[6] N. Bird, *A little peace of mind: the revolutionary solution for freedom from anxiety, panic attacks and stress* (2019), 10.

[7] E. Gilbert, *Big magic: creative living beyond fear* (2015), 34–36.

[8] Dr M. Grothe, *I never metaphor I didn't like: a comprehensive compilation of history's greatest analogies, metaphors, and similes* (2008).

ages by famous people. You're bound to find inspiration from them. How about these for starters:

- A friend is a present you give yourself. (Robert Louis Stevenson)

- Husbands are like fires. They go out when unattended. (Zsa Zsa Gabor)

- Life is always a tightrope or a feather bed. Give me the tightrope. (Edith Wharton)

Can you see how these metaphors and similes conjure up a visual image in your mind? They give a clarity and power to the concepts behind them that no straightforward description could ever achieve. When I think of a friend as being a present I give myself, I know what that means at an emotional level, not just a logical one.

You, we, they

There will be times when you describe what your readers should do, times when you talk about people generally and times when you include yourself. It can be confusing to know when to use 'you', 'they', and 'we'; which is the right one for each individual circumstance? Here's how I see the distinction.

You (for instance, 'You can tell when your sense of purpose has gone, because you feel listless and disorientated.') This is the best voice to use when you want your readers to sit up and take notice, because it's personal, active, and direct. It also encourages you to be specific about your points rather than to imply them, which can make a difference to how well you're understood. The 'You' voice is the one I've used most often throughout this book, and it's the one that I encourage you to default to as well.

We (for instance, 'When we ignore our kids, we make them feel hurt and abandoned.') This is a good option when you're saying something that might offend your readers if it was voiced as 'you', because when it's couched as 'we', it softens it. It's an inclusive and non-threatening way of putting across ideas that are personally challenging.

They (for instance, 'When people argue with their loved ones, they often lose their temper.') Although you may need to use this every now and then, it comes across as theoretical and indirect, so try to minimize it. Your readers won't feel as if you're talking to them personally.

Your visuals

In any self-help guide there's scope for diagrams, illustrations, lists, and charts. They're good not only for making things clear, but also for adding visual interest to your book. They can even give it character if you choose a unique and consistent style of illustration, as Steve Peters does in *The Chimp Paradox*.

So where should you use them? Wherever they'll add value. If something is hard to understand in writing, consider illustrating it with a chart or diagram; also, if you want to give an emotional quality to a point you're making, a drawing can help. Just bear in mind that illustrations don't work so well for e-books, so make sure they're not a substitute for your words but an addition to them.

What you put with it

Do you remember when you last learned a foreign language? I expect that the words sunk in most deeply when you put them into practice, rather than when you just read them in a textbook. In the same way, creating companion materials for your self-development guide can help your readers to gain clarity, because they give them a way of putting what they're learning into context.

What do I mean by companion materials? Anything that goes alongside your book and helps your readers to make more of the content. They can include workbooks, online materials such as videos and templates, and online courses. These can be downloadable, such as a pdf that asks people questions to fill in the answers to. I created a 'fill in the blanks' book planning template for my book *Your Business Your Book*, as a way of encouraging people to do the planning while they were reading about it. Not only has this proved beneficial to them, but I get to see who's downloaded it and have added them to my email list. If you like, you can expand this into a whole workbook that takes your readers from the beginning of your process to the end. Through this, you can challenge your readers to think more deeply about what they've read and give them space to expand upon it in a way that isn't possible just by reading the book.

And finally, what about an online course? This can help with understanding in so many ways. It enables you to bring your book to life with videos and visuals, and it gives you the opportunity to introduce yourself to your readers in 'person'. If you charge for the course, you can also expand your income.

You may be thinking, *Wait. I'm already writing a whole book and now she's expecting me to create all this other stuff as well?* Don't worry – none of this is compulsory. If you feel moved to do it, that's fine and good, and if you don't, it's not an issue. However, bear in mind that you can tackle it after you've sent your book to the publisher, because it doesn't have to be ready until the printed copies hit the shelves.

Now we'll look at the next step for clarity in your writing, which is how to be persuasive and engaging.

The landmarks

- There are three main ways to give your readers a clear and easy reading experience.
- The first is to organize your information in a way that motivates and informs them.
- The second is write it while putting yourself in their shoes.
- The third is to create companion materials that expand on or clarify the book that you've written.

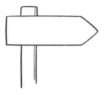

8. Be persuasive

I mentioned at the start of this book that one of the key weaknesses of some self-help guides is that they tell their readers what they should do, whereas people only do what they *want* to do. That means your challenge as an author is to get your readers to a place of wanting, and it's why persuasiveness needs to be at the core of your writing. Persuasiveness is the key to motivating your readers to set off on the journey you want them to take, and to making sure that they stay on it to the end.

You may be wondering: *Is being persuasive just another way of being manipulative? Is it a bit underhand? Why not just be up front about things?* I understand why you might have this concern, because as someone who works with people to improve their lives, it's important to you to be ethical. But there's a difference between persuasiveness and manipulation. Manipulation involves being coercive or deceptive, whereas persuasiveness is about leading people towards a goal in a transparent way. Your readers want to be motivated – in fact, they need it. If it was easy for them to change on their own, they wouldn't be reading your book.

Writing persuasively might seem like a tricky thing to do, but there are some principles and methods that will help you. Once you've reached the end of this chapter, you'll hopefully see that it's not the dark art you might have thought it was.

The genius of Aristotle

The Greek philosopher Aristotle coined what he called the three artistic proofs when it comes to communication. What I love about them is that they've stood the test of time, influencing how people write and speak today. They're essentially modes of persuasion and are called ethos, pathos, and logos.

Ethos: This is the ancient Greek word for 'character', and its relevance to writing lies in how you use it to show that you're a credible source of information.

Pathos: This is what generates emotion in readers, which is (as we'll learn) central to persuading anyone to do anything. That's why I'm going to spend the majority of this chapter exploring how you can include emotion in your book.

Logos: This is about reasoning and logic, or a method of persuading people through the use of facts and argument.

If you think about anything you've read that persuaded you to do or think about something differently, it almost certainly employed at least two of these three artistic proofs. It therefore follows that if you want to be persuasive in your writing, you need to use them too. Let's see what that entails.

Ethos (or credibility)

If you've ever spoken at an event or watched someone who has, you know the formula: before the speaker comes on stage, a compère introduces them by summarizing what qualifies them to be there. It might go something like this: 'Susan Wright has been helping people to find their inner spark for 15 years. After gaining a PhD in Psychology, she worked in the mental health system and then launched her own practice. These days, she focuses on bringing more joy into her client's lives, and she's here today to share some of her valuable insights with you. Please welcome Susan to the stage!'

Why does the compère do this? Because they know that if the people in the room are going to be motivated to listen to Susan, they have first to believe in her. If there's no belief, there's no trust, and if there's no trust, nothing that Susan says will make an impact. Therefore, one of the key ways in which Susan can create change in her audience is to ensure that her professional credentials are clear from the start.

If you think about your own experience of people who've tried to influence you in some way, I'm sure that one of the first questions you asked yourself was why you should believe them. And yet I'm often surprised by how reluctant some personal development authors are to showcase their expertise in their books. Maybe it's because they don't want to come across as arrogant and complacent. I'd certainly never recommend that, but what they're missing is the fact that their readers *want to know* what qualifies them to write about their subject. There's a huge difference between reading a book by someone who's clear about their experience and qualifications and someone who skirts around the subject. So it's vital that you make clear – up front and early on – what gives you the right to write your book.

Credentials can include:

- Your qualifications.

- Your experience of working with people using your expertise, both in terms of the number of years and the nature of it.

- Any standout accomplishments, either because of the results you achieved or because they were notably exciting or different.

- Your own experience of life and how it relates to the topic of your book.

I suggest that you use your book's introduction chapter to make it clear from the start why you're qualified to give advice (I cover how to write an introduction below). The other place you can do this is by having a 'The author' page.

Your 'The author' page

It sounds like a contradiction, but this page isn't about you, it's about your readers. What do they want to know about you? What are the key pieces of information that will help them to trust the advice you give? Qualifications and experience are important, but also an indication of what inspires your work. You can include testimonials, other books you've written, major talks you've delivered, or publicly available media that features you. Make sure that you include a reference to how people can find out more about you; this could be your website, social media, or an email address if you feel comfortable giving it out.

Write your 'The author' page in the third person (so it's 'he' or 'she', not 'I'), and in a warm and friendly tone. Ideally it will be a bit interesting and fun; it should make your readers want to learn more about your work. You also want them to feel that they're in safe hands, so it isn't the place to hold back on your credentials or get all modest. Go for it.

Your introduction chapter and 'The author' page aren't the only places that you can talk about your expertise; you can also drop it in throughout the book. One way of doing this is what I call 'seeding', which means inserting mini stories about your work into your narrative. For instance, if you help people coming up to retirement to create a plan for the rest of their lives, you might say: 'When I first start working with a client, I always begin by defining their goals for retirement, because I've found that retirees with goals are twice as likely to come up with a plan they're happy with than those who don't. That's why I'm starting with goals for you, too.' As long as you only do this occasionally and it's relevant to the topic you're covering, it's an excellent way of baking your expertise into your book.

Pathos (or the use of emotion)

We human beings are rational creatures. We weigh up options, consider choices, and steer away from rash decisions that we may later regret. Or so we like to think. In reality, our emotions play the primary role in our decision-making. If you don't believe me, try answering the following questions:

- Have you ever made a high-value, high-stakes purchase from a brand that you've never heard of, even if was at a great price?

- When you go to the supermarket, do you only ever buy the food that's on your list?

- Have you ever bought a car you hated the colour of and been completely okay about it?

If the answer to any or all of these is 'no', that's evidence of emotional decision-making. There's nothing wrong with it – we all do it. In fact, the only reason that we don't like admitting it is because reason and logic are so prized in Western culture. That's why we buy on emotion and justify with logic afterwards: 'Well, the car would've lost a lot of value with that horrible colour – it made sense to buy the silver one, even though it cost more.'

Purchase decisions are no different from other decisions; I only use examples of these because they're easy to relate to. When your readers look to you for help with making other choices about their lives – ones that have more far-reaching consequences than what to buy for dinner – they're also making them based on emotion. Which means that you must make judicious use of emotion-based persuasion in order to nudge them in the right direction.

In a book there are many ways that you can make your writing emotionally persuasive, and I'm going to focus on three key ones:

- Storytelling
- Empathy
- Interest

Storytelling

In their book about persuasive communication, *Made to Stick*, Chip and Dan Heath describe an exercise that they carry out with their Stanford students each year.[9] They give them some data about crime patterns in the US, after which half the students are asked to make a speech to their peers to convince them that crime is a serious problem. Each speaker is rated by their audience and, unsurprisingly, the most polished speakers

---

[9] C. Heath and D. Heath, *Made to stick: why some ideas survive and others die* 2008, 242–243.

tend to receive the highest marks. But then the audience members are asked to write down, for each speaker, what they *remember* about the talk that they heard. They're amazed to discover that, despite only a few minutes having elapsed since hearing the speeches, they can recall virtually none of the facts presented. What they can remember, though, are the stories that were in the speeches. In fact, 63% recall the stories and only 5% the individual statistics.

Who doesn't love a good story? I don't know about you, but I spend a fair bit of time and money on consuming stories. I read novels, watch films and TV series, go to plays, and listen to friends recounting the ups and downs of their lives. Why do I do that? Because there's a magnetic field around a story that pulls me in – I can't help but want to know what happens next.

It's been discovered that there are scientific reasons for our fascination with stories. Among other things, they stimulate the release of oxytocin, which is a hormone generated when we snuggle up with someone we love or interact with friends; it helps us to feel close to them. That's why we feel as if we have a relationship with the characters in a novel, even though we know they're made up. Oxytocin is a powerful drug; it's even been shown that people with high levels of it are 48% more likely to donate to charity than those without.[10] If it can do that, then surely it can give someone the motivation to change career, transform their relationship or overcome their phobia?

As we saw from the Stanford experiment above, there's another reason why stories are persuasive, which is that they make the information within them memorable. What sticks in your mind for longer: facts and figures alone, or when they're embedded in a story? Suppose you're a weight-loss coach and you have

---

[10] www.researchgate.net/publication/51149904_Oxytocin_infusion_increases_charitable_donations_regardless_of_monetary_resources

evidence that people who lose only two pounds a week keep the weight off in the long term more successfully than those who lose more.[11] That's certainly a persuasive statistic, and there's nothing wrong with putting it in your book (it's great for 'logos', or reason, as we'll explore soon). But by the time your readers have finished the final chapter, will they remember it? Has it lodged in their brains and – just as importantly – influenced their behaviour? Probably not.

How much more persuasive would it be to build the statistic into a narrative?

Mary had been trying to lose weight for years; she'd tried diet after diet and managed to shift a dress size, but in the end she always put the pounds back on. It was so unfair, especially given that her sister could eat anything she wanted without putting on an inch. Until the day she started working with me, that is (see how good this story is for your credibility, too?). I discovered that she'd been starving herself and losing six pounds a week on average, which was way too much for permanent weight loss – nor was it safe. It took a while to convince Mary that, by eating more, she'd lose less weight in the short term but have better results in the long run. In fact, at first she refused to believe me and carried on with her drastic regime. But one day she felt dizzy with hunger and almost crashed her car. This prompted her to re-evaluate her diet and she started to see the sense in what I'd been telling her. So, while she wasn't sure whether it would work, she decided to give it a go. The result was that she discovered it was so much nicer eating sensibly that she stuck with the new diet. Nine months later, she reached her ideal weight and three years further on, she's still there.

---

[11] I have no idea if this is true – it's a made-up example to illustrate my point. Don't take dieting advice from me!

After reading Mary's story, I'd be willing to bet that your readers would consider following her example.

There's one further reason why stories are persuasive, as novelist and writer Will Storr explains in his book *The Science of Storytelling*, and it's a pretty deep one.[12] It's because, as Storr puts it, 'story is what brain does'. If you cast your mind back to the last few films or novels that you've consumed, you'll realize that, at the beginning of any gripping tale, something surprising and unfair often happens to the main character. The rest of the story consists of their quest to regain control over their life. This is how we feel about our own lives, too. None of us like to think of ourselves as a being victim of circumstance with no ability to influence what happens to us, so by reading a story about someone like Mary, who overcomes her problem by making a change to her weight-loss regime, we feel more in control ourselves. We identify with her struggle and feel inspired by her solution, which reassures us that we too have the ability to change.

How to tell a story

There are whole books written on the art of storytelling, so please don't feel pressured to become some kind of expert storyteller overnight. It's simple, persuasive stories that you want to write, not *War and Peace*. With that in mind, here are the five basic elements your story needs to include if it's to be a great read and convince people about the point you want to make.

It must be about one significant problem

You're using your story to persuade your readers to change one thing, so don't confuse them by adding in lots of problems.

---

[12] W. Storr, *The science of storytelling* 2019, 3.

Also, the issue should seem difficult or impossible to solve; easy problems aren't interesting to read about. Mary's was that she wanted to lose weight quickly *and* keep it off in the long term, even though this had never worked for her in the past – that's a tall order.

The problem should come across as unfair to the main character

All problems are unfair when they happen to us, aren't they? Why can't we go through life without them? Why, why, why [stamps foot]? What's more, the perceived unfairness of the situation in a book is central to how much we relate to the main character. To Mary it seemed wrong that her sister could eat as much as she wanted but that she couldn't. How was that okay?

The difficulty of solving the problem pushes the main character outside of their comfort zone

When you're trying to motivate someone to make a change in their life, there are reasons why they've not done it already. Maybe they didn't know what to do, but it's just as likely that they had an inkling and yet lacked the impetus to make the shift. Change is painful, so your protagonist should also find it hard. What's the comfort zone that your readers are in and that your main character could dramatize for them? Mary had to consider that the sacrifices she'd made for years to lose weight were in fact what was helping to increase it. At first this was psychologically too difficult for her to accept, especially as her efforts had produced impressive short-term results.

Trying to solve the problem causes more problems

Because we don't like being outside our comfort zone, we'll do anything to avoid it. But that won't help us to solve our problem, in fact it often makes it worse. It should be the same for your main character: by trying to find alternative solutions that are easier for them to accept than the dreaded stepping outside of the comfort zone, they only exacerbate the original issue. In Mary's case, she carried on starving herself because she was too invested in her drastic diet regime to consider doing otherwise.

A final battle resolves the problem

So strong can be our attachment to our preferred solutions (even if they don't work) that it usually takes something dramatic to shift them. This is the final battle, after which we've 'won' and can celebrate our success. In Mary's case it took almost crashing her car for her to see that there might be a better way to lose weight, but once she made a leap of faith and started eating more sensibly, she eventually gained her reward.

Questions about writing stories

When I coach my clients in the art of writing stories for their self-help guides, I'm often asked questions, so I've answered some of them here to help you.

I don't know any stories that contain those five criteria. What do I do?

You probably do, it's just that you've never thought about them like that before. However, don't be afraid to embellish or alter your stories a little if it makes them more engaging. Or you could combine two or three stories into a more convincing one. You're telling the story in the service of encouraging your readers to make important changes in their lives – it's okay not to stick rigidly to the facts.

You mean my stories don't have to be real?

Mary the dieter isn't real, and her story still works for this book. In fact, some of the most compelling stories I've created while ghostwriting books have been purely to illustrate a point. I've even included overarching stories, either in instalments per chapter or in one go at the end, which show the journey of a fictional person who followed the advice in the book. I'd never claim that a story really happened if it didn't, but there's nothing wrong with making one up if it suits your purposes. Just be up front about it.

What if I want to write about a client and maintain their confidentiality at the same time?

If your client doesn't want to be named in the book that's understandable, but you can change their name and enough details of the story to make them unrecognizable. As long as no one can identify them from what you've included, their anonymity is preserved. And as a separate note, client success stories are an excellent seeding device. They add to your credibility and show that your book is based on real-world situations.

Can I write stories about myself?

Of course! If your personal experience is relevant to a point you're making and would be the basis for a good story, go ahead. Just make sure that you include your struggle, along with any mistakes and setbacks and what you learned from them – they make you more relatable.

I have some long stories and case studies. Should I separate them out in the text?

If they're long and not directly relevant to the point you're making at that moment, it's best to separate them out using a visual device such as a shaded or outlined block. If they're not, including them in the narrative is the better option.

Empathy

If storytelling is the first (and most complex) method for stimulating your readers' emotions, the second is empathy. It's a truism that in order to understand what someone is telling us, we first need to feel understood; the phrase 'they don't care what you know until they know that you care' is spot on. So it's essential to show your readers that you appreciate their problem and understand where they're coming from – they need to be sure that you 'see' them.

It's also important to acknowledge that their problem isn't their fault. I know that might not fit with the way you see it – after all, every issue is in some way to do with what we've said or done in the past. But we only do what makes sense to us at the time; if your readers have been arguing with their family for years, that was only because there seemed to be no other way. The important thing is that they now want to change the situation, and it's reassuring for them to abandon any self-blame they may have. The day they start reading your book is the day they begin to change.

What if you're a 'tell it like it is' kind of person? Someone who doesn't feel comfortable with being touchy-feely on the page, or in real life? That's fine, and I expect that your strength as a coach or therapist lies in your no-nonsense way of giving advice. But remember that when you're speaking with someone in person you can soften your communication through tone of voice and body language, so people can see that your words are coming from a place of care. In writing it's not so easy, so you may have to find other ways of making it clear that you understand your readers' problems and where they come from.

Interest

The final reason for using pathos (or emotion) for persuasion is to ensure that you gain and keep your readers' interest throughout the book. It's a process that starts at the beginning, with your introduction chapter, and carries on all the way through to your conclusion.

Your introduction chapter

This is probably the most important chapter in your book, because it's the one that will make or break your readers' decision to read it. Due to the ease of checking out your first few pages on Amazon's 'Look Inside' feature, it even influences whether they buy it in the first place. One thing's for certain: your readers won't read a boring introduction and then convince themselves that it's worth ploughing on with the rest of the book. Their lives are too busy and their attention spans too short for that.

Which brings me to the central purpose of your introduction chapter: to capture your readers' interest and earn their trust. What it's *not* for is to talk at length about your book's topic or to tell people why you wrote it. At this stage, all your readers want to know is the following:

- What's in it for me to read this book?
- Is it aimed at someone like me?
- What kind of experience am I going to have when I read it?

That's it – it's pretty simple. So how do you write an introduction that works? Here's a helpful framework:

- Tell your readers in your first few lines what problem you'll be solving. They want to know up front whether your book will help them.
- Empathize with your readers, showing that you appreciate their pain. At the same time, make it clear

that you're familiar with who they are, because they need to feel confident that this book is for them. You should be happy for the 'wrong' readers to leave you at this point.

- Briefly present your solution or explanation. This is the 'gold' in your book.

- Explain your credibility, or ethos: what makes you qualified to write about this topic?

- Tell your readers what journey the book will be taking them on and what kind of trip it will be. Be concrete and make a big promise.

- Encourage them to read on now – create a sense of urgency.

Keeping the interest alive

You've grabbed people's attention with your introduction chapter; now you need to keep it throughout the ones that follow. There are countless ways of doing that and many of them are covered throughout this book, but the one that I'll focus on here is especially relevant to self-help guides: interactive exercises and quizzes.

Some authors are sceptical about these and assume that few people bother with them. They may be right, and there will always be a proportion of refuseniks who prefer to carry on reading than stop and think. However, that's because it's unusual to find interactive elements that are well thought through. Often they're vaguely worded, give little sense of how they help people, or are too complicated and time-consuming for someone who's in the middle of a reading experience. You're asking someone to interrupt themselves to do something that takes a mental effort, so you must make it worth their while. Here are some tips for high-quality interaction.

Ensure that the interactivity has a clear purpose. When I first started reading Lois Frankel's *Nice Girls Don't Get Rich*, I remember thinking that I wasn't like the women her book was aimed at – the ones who didn't have much idea about their finances.[13] But after I completed the self-assessment quiz at the beginning, I realized that I wasn't quite as savvy as I thought. It was a humbling moment, and one that set me up to read the rest of the book with an open mind.

What purpose do your interactive exercises or quizzes have? Are they designed to lead to a specific outcome that's relevant to the part of the book they're in? It's important not to include them for the sake of it, but only where they'll help your readers to make sense of what you're teaching them.

Explain the benefits and process. Remember '*Why? What? How? What if?*' from Chapter 6? Make sure that you cover off the purpose of the exercise – what your readers will get out of it. Then clearly explain what they should do, as a numbered list of actions if appropriate. After that, give details about how they should go about it (if it's not obvious) and then talk them through what to do about the results. What's different for them now? How could they apply what they've learned outside of the book?

If interactivity is essential to you, build your book around it. Layla Saad does this powerfully in *Me and White Supremacy*. Her aim is to enable white people to recognize their privilege so that they're better placed to combat racism. She achieves this through a 28-day programme, with each chapter talking about a specific aspect of racism and ending with a series of questions and challenges for the reader to reflect on. Everything that

---

[13] L.P. Frankel, *Nice girls don't get rich: 75 avoidable mistakes women make with money* (2005), 6–13.

comes before the exercises is leading up to them, so in that sense they're the central focus of the book.

Your conclusion

If the purpose of your introduction chapter is to motivate your readers to start the book, your conclusion chapter is there to give a satisfying ending to it. There are three main ways you can approach this.

Summarize what they've learned. This is the final piece of the 'tell 'em' sandwich that I mentioned earlier. It's your readers' final chance to get their heads around your book in a top-line way, absorbing its main messages in one place. It's valuable because people need to read something more than once before it sinks in.

Inspire them to feel excited about the future. Your readers have come to your book with the hope of improving something in their lives, but for them to feel motivated to make the necessary changes they need a vision of what life will look like afterwards. Your conclusion is an opportunity for you to paint that picture so they can see themselves at the end of their journey, transformed for the better.

Encourage them to put what they've learned into practice. This is a helpful place to ask your readers to make a practical plan for how they're going to shift their behaviour. It could involve deciding what they're going to tackle first, second, and third; the situations they're going to focus on; or the further reading or exploration that they could do.

Logos (or reason)

This is the final element of the persuasive ethos, pathos, logos trilogy. Logos refers to facts or logic, which can be valuable tools for bringing people over to your way of thinking. Not only that, but logos can also add to your ethos (or credibility and authority), because it shows that you've read widely around your topic and have been exposed to expert opinions. Here are a couple of ways to use logos in your book.

Explain your research

When you quote research by people who have credibility in that area, you're borrowing some of their ethos for yourself. Instead of it being only you who says that something is true, you're backing yourself up with findings from others. If you reference research, it's important that you credit the researcher and the report; if possible, add a footnote so that your readers can access the full version if they want to.

Quote facts, figures, and statistics

In *Yes! 50 Scientifically Proven Ways to Be Persuasive*, Robert B. Cialdini tells a story that has stayed with me ever since I read it.[14] It's about the problems experienced by the management of the Petrified Forest in Arizona. Some visitors to the forest had a habit of taking irreplaceable pieces of wood as keepsakes, and the management's intention was to prevent it. Cialdini and his team set up three trials. In one, they put up a sign stating: 'Many past visitors have removed the petrified wood from the park, changing the natural state of the Petrified Forest.' In the second, the sign said: 'Please don't remove the petrified wood from the park, in order to preserve the natural state of the Petrified Forest.' The third trial involved no sign at all. They then placed marked pieces of petrified wood along the visitor pathways to monitor how many were stolen.

---

[14] N.J. Goldstein, S.J. Martin and R.B. Cialdini, *Yes! 50 scientifically proven ways to be persuasive* (2010), 20–23.

The results? In the first trial ('Many past visitors'), 7.92% of the pieces were taken; in the second ('Please don't remove') it was only 1.67%, and in the third (no sign) it was 2.92%. The conclusion that Cialdini drew from this was that telling people they'd be part of the 'many' if they were to steal wood encouraged them to do just that. In fact, it was worse than saying nothing at all. Therefore, if the forest management wanted to encourage people to leave the wood alone, they should emphasize the fact that this was what the majority of park visitors did.

The reason I mention this story isn't to give a lesson in the psychology of herd mentality and its role in persuasion, useful though it is for that too. It's to show you that facts, figures, and statistics are hard to ignore. It's their irrefutability that does it – they're not your subjective opinions, but objectively true. You won't persuade people by using them alone because they're most powerful when combined with stories and emotion (I'd never have remembered the exact figures if I hadn't gone back to look them up), but you'll go a long way towards neutralizing any scepticism your readers may have.

Being persuasive is one of the most powerful tools in your kit for writing a successful self-help book, but winning your readers over to your point of view isn't the only reason you're writing it. You also want to allow your readers to get to know you, which is what we'll look at next.

The landmarks

- Writing persuasively is essential if you're to bring your readers around to your way of thinking.
- Establishing your credibility gives your readers a reason to trust your advice.

- Stimulating the right emotions encourages your readers to effect the change that's right for them. You can do this through storytelling, showing empathy, and gaining (and keeping) their interest.

- Backing up your assertions with facts and figures adds weight and objectivity to them.

9. Be you

Have a read of these two extracts from different self-help guides.

From *Big Magic: Creative Living Beyond Fear*, by Elizabeth Gilbert.[15]

> The patron goddess of creative success can sometimes seem like a rich, capricious old lady who lives in a giant mansion on a distant hill and who makes really weird decisions about who gets her fortune. She sometimes rewards charlatans and ignores the gifted. She cuts people out of her will who loyally served her for their entire lives, and then gives a Mercedes to that cute boy who cut her lawn once. She changes her mind about things. We try to divine her motives, but they remain occult. She is never obliged to explain herself to us. In short, the goddess of creative success may show up for

---

[15] E. Gilbert, *Big magic: creative living beyond fear* (2015).

you, or she may not. Probably best, then, if you don't count on her, or attach your definition of personal happiness to her whims.

From *The Subtle Art of Not Giving a F*ck*, by Mark Manson.[16]

Now here's the problem: our society today, through the wonders of consumer culture and hey-look-my-life-is-cooler-than-yours social media, has bred a whole generation of people who believe that having these negative experiences – anxiety, fear, guilt, etc. – is totally not okay. I mean, if you look at your Facebook feed, everybody there is having a fucking grand old time. Look, eight people got married this week! And some sixteen-year-old on TV got a Ferrari for her birthday. And another kid just made two billion dollars inventing an app that automatically delivers you more toilet paper when you run out. Meanwhile, you're stuck at home flossing your cat.

Apart from marvelling at how each author has made their advice come alive through the use of metaphors and stories, how do you think that the extracts compare in tone and voice? Both are to the point, delivering hard-to-accept truths in a humorous way, but they do it differently. Elizabeth Gilbert's passage is full of understated humour and comes across as caring, literary, and thoughtful; you can almost see her delivering it while sitting on a sofa, giving advice to a friend. Mark Manson's, however, takes a more bullish approach; in my mind I see him holding forth in a bar, drink in hand, while he regales anyone who will listen with his advice.

---

[16] M. Manson, *The subtle art of not giving a f*ck* (2016).

These differences are important, because when we read a personal development book we're not just learning new stuff, we're also getting to know the author. What kind of person are they? Can we trust them? Would we want to work with them as a client one day? That's why your book should lift the lid on who you are. You might find this idea a little exposing but don't worry, I'm not suggesting that you reveal your innermost personal secrets (although you can if you want to – that would say something about your personality in itself). What I'm getting at is that it's helpful if your book reads as if it's from you and not from anyone else. And this comes down to your book's voice and tone.

Your voice

Your writing voice is how you use language; the things you say that are unique to you – those word combinations that are yours alone. When you've found your voice, it becomes one of your greatest assets as an author, because it's what animates the stories you tell and the advice you give. It makes them come alive.

There's a huge amount of advice out there about how to find your 'writing voice' (I know, I've looked). But honestly, I think that most of it makes the process seem more complicated than it really is. You don't need to read a lot of articles or do countless exercises to find your voice; you only need to focus on the following.

How you speak

You're used to talking to clients, so the next time you're writing some advice in your book, just try wording it as you'd speak to them. When you've finished you'll need to formalize it, making the passage grammatically correct and substituting some words with others so that the sentences flow. You might even need to move your sentences around. But whatever you end up with will sound more authentically you than if you'd ignored the speaking part of your voice.

Where you stand

Where are you positioning yourself in relation to your readers? Are you a cheerleader, encouraging them from the sidelines? A leader, drawing them forwards from the front? Or standing next to them, with a hand around their shoulders? You can see how your tone of voice should reflect the kind of relationship you want to have with them. If it's a cheerleader, you'll want to be upbeat and positive; if it's a leader, you'll want to be authoritative; and if you're standing alongside your readers, you'll want to be friendly and encouraging.

Of course, you might take any of these approaches at different places in your book – in fact you probably should. It would be a dull book that employed only one stance all the way through. But thinking about where you stand can be a big help in forming your voice, because it tells you a lot about how you see your relationship with your readers.

The words and phrases you love

We each of us have our favoured ways of expressing ourselves. Hold on to yours – they're precious. Don't ever feel that you must give up on who you are in order to fit a template of what you assume a self-help book writer is supposed to sound like. I find this happens a lot with my book coaching clients at first; they can sometimes write in a stiff and formal way. It's understandable, because they have a vision of their most feared schoolteacher standing over their shoulder, red pen twitching. But what really draws your readers to your work is when you abandon the 'bookish' approach and speak to them as human beings instead.

If you look at the two extracts with which I started this chapter, you can see what I mean about word choice. Elizabeth Gilbert's vocabulary is relatively literary, with words such as 'capricious' and 'charlatans' making an appearance. She's assuming that her readers know what they mean and isn't afraid to mix them up with everyday words and phrases like 'cute' and 'She changes her mind about things'. Mark Mason's approach is more colloquial throughout; he uses words like 'okay', 'etc.', and the ever-present 'fucking'. His phrases are also more conversational, such as when he writes: 'some sixteen-year-old... And another kid...' The point is that after reading even a short extract from these books we feel as if we've become acquainted with their authors because they expressed themselves in a way that was right for them.

You might be wondering whether it's okay for some of your readers not to like your distinctive voice. What if it turns them off? I can appreciate that this might be uncomfortable for you but think about it this way: you'll never please every reader. It's far more important to speak directly to the ones who 'get' you and who might want to work with you after they've finished your book, than it is to cater for all potential readers. Hiding your personality never pays dividends in the long run.

What are your favourite words and phrases? Try writing them down in a list, without judgement. It's normal to feel a little insecure about the vocabulary we use day to day because it can seem pedestrian, but that's only because it's familiar to us. To others, it might be just what they need to help them get to know us.

Your tone

You have a long-awaited evening planned with a friend this weekend and are looking forward to it. An hour before you're due to leave the house, you receive this text message: *I can't see you tonight, let's rearrange.*

It sounds a bit cold and rude, doesn't it? But what if they'd written this instead?

Really sorry, something's come up and I can't make it anymore. What a pain. Can you do Tuesday instead?

Now you're feeling more understood. The difference between the two is in the tone, which in turn is created by the choice of words and the sentence structure. Your book's tone is important because it generates the 'mood' of your book, thereby influencing how people feel when they're reading it. And given that pathos, with its emotional charge, is one of the three keys to being persuasive, these feelings are a part of your book's potential for success.

You'll create a tone whether you try to or not, so it's worth making sure that it's the one you want. Many successful self-help guides have an upbeat tone because they want their readers to feel enthusiastic about change; when we feel positive, we're more likely to entertain the idea of doing things differently. Sometimes this can be achieved through humour, but more often it's created through the use of everyday language, short and simple sentences, and the sense of commitment to their readers that the author puts across. So how does this work?

- Vocabulary – is it everyday, formal, literary, or casual?
- Phrases – are they standard, convoluted, short and sharp?
- Punctuation – are your sentences long and flowing, or short and to the point?
- Metaphors and visuals – are they humorous, outlandish, traditional, innovative, or something else?

An often-overlooked way of creating a mood or tone is through illustrations. *The Chimp Paradox* by Steve Peters contains drawings that look deliberately amateurish in order to make the book feel accessible, while other books, such as *Women Don't Owe You Pretty* by Florence Given, use colour images that provide the entire backdrop to the book. It would be impossible to imagine it without them.

If you're wondering how to put all this into practice, it's worth knowing that tone and voice can be hard to pin down, and you can waste a lot of time trying to analyze them to the nth degree. I suggest that you don't try too hard at first – just write what feels right, then go back later and revise. We'll cover this in the next chapter when we come to editing your book.

The landmarks

- The voice and tone in which you write your book has a fundamental impact on how your messages are received.

- Your writing voice is influenced by how you speak, the standpoint you take in relation to your readers, and the words and phrases you use.

- Your book's tone creates the mood of your book and comes from the type of language and visuals you employ.

PUT YOUR BOOK OUT THERE: ARRIVE AT YOUR DESTINATION

10. Edit your book

During the travels that I've been on throughout my life, one of the discoveries I've made is that the most fun and memorable journeys are those in which not everything goes according to plan; a certain amount of course correction is needed to make them stand out. In the same way, the first version of your book isn't the one that will be ready to publish – it will require adjustments, trimming, and new additions. Good editing is part of good writing, so my aim here is to give you a simple process for polishing your manuscript.

When to edit

After you've written your first chapter, it can be tempting to revise it before you go any further. I'm going to suggest that's a bad idea, for various reasons:

- You'll lose the momentum for keeping going with your book.

- You won't do a good job of editing if you haven't written the whole book yet – you need to see it in its entirety to know what's working and what isn't.

- It's an amazing moment when you see the first draft of your whole book, so why delay it?

Keep on keeping on until you reach the end. Have the courage to accept that what you've drafted at first will be far from perfect, but that you have full permission to make as many changes as you like when you've done it.

How to edit

Although you can write your first draft in whatever order you like, it's helpful to have a process for editing. When you have 50,000 words to wrangle into shape, it's easy to get confused with where you're up to or what you need to do next, so make life easier for yourself by taking it step by step.

Step 1: get ready

Give yourself at least a couple of weeks between finishing your first draft and starting the editing process. You need space to forget what you've written so that you're coming to it afresh. The beauty of this is that you'll experience all kinds of surprises, such as: 'I'm a genius!' and 'What was I thinking?' or even, 'Who wrote this sh*t?' Don't deny yourself the pleasure of these spontaneous reactions – not only are they a joy, but they also tell you what needs to change.

Next, print out your manuscript, numbering the pages and starting each chapter on a new one. I know, the trees, but when we read on a screen, we skim the pages and don't see all the things we need to. And while you're about it, allow yourself a sense of smug satisfaction when you see that pile of paper in front of you. Because it was you who created it – yes, you.

Your final job for this step is to get hold of some sticky notes, a pen and some blank sheets of A4 paper. Write the name of each chapter across the top of a separate sheet; you'll be sticking your notes below it. Now find yourself a comfortable spot away from your desk to read your book.

Step 2: put your brain into gear

Go back to your original aim, topic, and target readership. Remind yourself why you're writing this book, who it's for and what its 'gold' is. What's the point of your self-help guide? How will it benefit its readers? Jot your answers on a blank sheet of paper and keep it beside you at all times as you edit – it will be your sense checker for whenever you feel unsure about something.

Step 3: edit for content

Here you're editing not for style, but for content. Take one chapter at a time and, before you start reading it, note down brief answers to the following questions on your chapter sheets:

- What's the purpose of this chapter?
- If my readers took away only one point from it, what would I want it to be?
- What do I want them to know and feel by the end?

Now read through, using the following pointers to guide you:

- Does anything in this chapter not serve its purpose? If not, cross it out or make a note to move it somewhere more useful by jotting a remark on a sticky note and placing it on your chapter heading sheet.

- Are your points ordered in a way that makes sense for your readers? If not, draw some arrows to reorder them.

- Have you used *Why? What? How? What if?* for all your main points? This will ensure that you're not falling into the trap of just telling your readers what to do.

- Have you included enough (or too much) information, given your readers' level of knowledge?

- Have you referred to anything coming later or earlier in the book? If so, don't try to find it now, but jot it on a sticky note and place it under that chapter heading on your sheet. You'll use it to check for consistency later.

- Have you repeated stories or points from other chapters? If you think you might have done, note these on your sticky notes and check later.

- If it occurs to you that new material needs to be added, write it on a blank sheet of paper and insert it into the relevant place in your manuscript.

- Do you need to do more research on an area? Could you add any case studies or stories? If so, this goes on a sticky note too.

Step 4: make your changes

Return to your computer and make the necessary changes, saving the chapters as a second draft. You can bin the sticky notes as you go along (woohoo!). While you're rewriting, stay alert for further changes that you might need to make, but avoid worrying about how things are worded; you're focusing on top-line flow of content here.

Step 5: edit for style

Print out your manuscript once more and find your comfy chair again. This time, you're focusing more on what your book is like to read, rather than what it says. To get a feel for that, read it aloud. It's the only reliable way to gain an objective view of the rhythm of your writing, because when something snags for you, it will also snag for your readers. Reading aloud is something that most authors don't bother with, but when you do it you'll see why it makes such a difference.

You can use the following as a checklist for making sure that your book is a delight to read:

- **Is it clear?** Are you using plain English, or have you slipped into complicated language or jargon? Have you spotted any woolly phrases, or words that don't add anything but are there for the sake of it? Do you have headings and subheadings where appropriate?

- **Is it a good read?** Do you find your mind wandering? If you're bored, your readers will be too. Is your writing too long-winded? Or could it do with a story, an interesting fact, or a touch of controversy to liven it up? Are you using metaphors and analogies to avoid a dry reading experience?

- **Is it persuasive?** Remember ethos, pathos, and logos. Have you included:

  ○ Evidence of your credibility and authority in your subject matter?

  ○ Stories?

  ○ Empathy?

  ○ Research, facts, and figures if they help to convince your readers?

  ○ Interactive exercises if appropriate?

  ○ An introduction chapter that encourages people to read the book?

○ A conclusion chapter that helps understanding and inspires your readers for the future?

Use the same process for additions and corrections as for Step 3, then return to your computer and input your changes. Give yourself a break and then reread the entire manuscript one more time (on screen this time if you prefer), tweaking as you go along. Finally, collapse in a heap/pour yourself a drink/go wild with excitement in whatever excessive way that works for you – you've earned it.

Beta readers

There's another step in finishing your book that happens before you make the final changes I mentioned above, and that's to send it to some beta readers. This is a test group of people who read your draft manuscript and give you feedback, so that you can make sure it's the best it can be before your book is published. It's an optional step but it's worth considering for the following reasons.

Your book will be better

When you're an expert in something, no matter how hard you try to put yourself in the shoes of someone who knows little about it, you'll make some wrong assumptions. You might skip a vital element because you assume that your readers are more knowledgeable than they are and, because you're already fascinated by the topic, you might not think to include things that keep your readers' attention. Is your book structured in a way that makes sense? Do your analogies work? Do people find it clear and persuasive? You'll only find out by asking your beta readers.

It's a dry run for publishing

Until I came to the end of writing my first book, *Your Business Your Book*, I'd never fully understood the pre-publication jitters that my ghostwriting and coaching clients went through. Now I do – and they're awful. I had the same questions going around in my head: *Is this book any good? What will people think? Will it sell?* It's enough to keep any author awake at night.

However, the bonus of having your book beta-read is that it's a 'soft publish'. It gives you the experience of putting your manuscript out there to be judged, but privately and only by a few people; this gets you used to the idea of being a published author. You'll also feel more confident about your book when you know that it's been critiqued and you've made changes as a result. People can tell the difference between an author who's sure of their work and one who isn't, so this makes a real difference.

You can build a fan base

As the first people to see your book, your beta readers make up a select bunch. They've had the chance to become involved with your author journey and will almost certainly be happy to help you promote your book at launch. It can be invaluable to have a small team of cheerleaders at that time (and remember to thank them in your acknowledgements page).

How to set up your beta readers

Hopefully I've convinced you that it's worth the effort of enlisting beta-reading help, but how do you know who to ask? It's easiest to start with who *not* to ask. The ideal beta reader is not your spouse, mum, or best friend; neither is it another expert in your field. In the case of the latter, they're too close to your subject matter, and in the case of the former, they'll only tell you what you want to hear. No one loves being informed by their husband or wife that their first chapter doesn't make sense; even if you say that you want honest advice, you really don't.

Instead, your beta readers should be those who represent the kind of people you envisage reading your book when it's published. Think of those in your circle who have similar problems to your readers. Could you picture them choosing to read your book? If so, you're on the right lines.

Try exploring these areas, aiming for around half a dozen readers in total:

- Past and current clients
- People on your email list
- Trusted colleagues and connections
- Friends

Everyone has beta readers available to them, they just don't always know it.

What to ask your beta readers

It's helpful for your beta readers if they know what kind of feedback you want. Suggested questions to ask them are:

- What main message did you take from the book?
- Where did I skimp on detail and where did I give too much?
- Was there anything that confused you?
- Was there anything that bored you?
- What did you enjoy?
- Is there anything else that you'd like to tell me?

You'll receive a wide range of comments, many of which will be positive and a few negative. Welcome the negatives as if they're your best friends because they help you to improve. And the positives? Store them away for when you need a pre-publication nerves settler – they'll be like gold dust then.

You'll have to decide which improvements to make and which to let go. If you receive similar feedback from more than one person, you can pretty much guarantee that it's solid. However, many suggestions will be one-offs, and it's up to you whether you want to action them. I've made changes based on beta feedback from only one person if I can see that it made sense, but if I've felt strongly about keeping things as they were, I've ignored it.

You've reached a landmark moment: you're ready to publish your book. In the next chapter we'll explore the various publishing options so that you can decide which one is right for you.

The landmarks

- Don't edit your book until you've reached the end of your first draft.

- Using a solid process for editing avoids confusion and will give you a good result.

- Beta readers help you to improve your manuscript and give you confidence when it comes to publication.

11. Publish your book

In my conversations with prospective authors, I find that one of their dilemmas is how to get their books published. This is understandable, because when you don't have any experience of the publishing industry it can seem like a bit of a minefield. I'm here to tell you that it's not as complicated as you might think and that there are options for making publishing easy for yourself that you may not be aware of. While not being an exhaustive explanation of the publishing process, this chapter gives you the main things that you need to know.

What is publishing?

First of all, what does publishing involve? That might sound like a strange question because we all know what a book is, but are you aware of what it takes to put a book onto the shelves? There are multiple tasks:

- Copy-editing your manuscript (checking your spelling and grammar, making sure that everything makes sense, and ensuring that you've presented your writing consistently).
- Designing your book cover.
- Writing your back cover blurb.
- Purchasing an ISBN (International Standard Book Number).
- Creating the metadata for your book (the information about it that sits within the ISBN).
- Formatting the interior layout of the book.
- Proofreading the formatted manuscript.
- Creating an e-book version, and maybe an audio book as well.
- Printing copies.
- Uploading to online retailers and sending copies to distribution warehouses.
- Listing with book wholesalers.

This isn't a comprehensive list. There are many other things that publishers potentially do, depending on the type they are. This includes professional advice on publishing strategy, developmental editing, advice on positioning and marketing, foreign rights sales, and lots of other responsibilities.

Now that you know what publishing involves, what options are available to you? There are three, each with their own pros and cons:

- Traditional publishing
- Paid-for publishing
- Self-publishing

Traditional publishing

This is what most people think of when they hear the word 'publishing'. It's making your book available through a publishing house such as Penguin Random House, Simon & Schuster, Macmillan, or through the plethora of smaller publishers that also exist. The differentiating factor with traditional publishing is that it's up to the publisher whether they accept your book, rather than for you to decide whether they publish it. For them to be interested, they'll want to be satisfied that it fulfils the following criteria.

It's commercially viable: to a traditional publisher, your book is a product that they'll manufacture and sell, so they want one they can shift in large enough numbers to make the financial risk worthwhile.

It's aimed at the right audience for them: some publishers specialize in mass market books, others in niche titles. Even the latter will want to be sure that they can sell thousands of copies, though.

It's written by an author with a strong marketing platform: a traditional publisher will look to see how large your personal audience is before they consider signing you. Do you already have an email list and a social media following consisting of multiple thousands? Do you regularly speak at large events? Are you willing to spend your own time and money on promoting your book to the right people and at volume? The marketing of your book will be largely your job, and although your publisher might support you, they prefer to go with authors who are a sure bet.

How do they decide whether you and your manuscript fit the bill? You send them a proposal, which is essentially a sales document for your book. It's a significant undertaking in its own right and you'll probably need some support with writing it; there are books that guide you through, or you can enlist the help of a book coach or ghostwriter with experience of the publishing industry.

Is traditional publishing an option for you? It's worth considering these pros and cons.

The pros of traditional publishing

Prestige: there's an unwritten assumption that, if you've landed a traditional deal, your book must be of high quality. There's some truth in this, because traditional publishers have high standards and accept only a fraction of the manuscripts they receive.

Validation: it's natural to have doubts about your book, so being acquired by an agent or publisher can be a confidence-booster.

No cost to you: the publisher pays for the cover design, typesetting, print, and all other tasks and costs associated with putting your book into the world.

Breadth of distribution: you're more likely to see your book on the shelves of physical bookstores than the other publishing routes.

Some marketing: the publisher will help with this, although most of your book marketing will be down to you.

The cons of traditional publishing

Time to market: publishers and agents reject the vast majority of the proposals that they receive, and it can take several months (if ever) to hear back from them. After that, waiting many more months for your book to appear isn't unusual. If you want your book to start earning its keep straightaway, this isn't for you.

Changing times: it's no longer the case that readers judge a book by its publisher. Think of your favourite self-help guide right now, without looking at it. Can you tell me who published it?

Loss of copyright: you have to license this to your publisher, so might not be able to use your book's content for your own purposes.

Lack of ownership: your book isn't 'yours' anymore. Do you want to decide your own title and cover design? You can give an opinion, but it's not your decision. You'll also have to make changes to your manuscript to match the publisher's requirements.

Low royalties: there's a wide range, but they're way lower than with the other publishing options (and advances are rare). Also, some publishers expect you to buy a quantity of your books to sell yourself.

Self-publishing

If you look at the list of publishing tasks at the beginning of this chapter, you can see that these are the things you'll need to do yourself if you're to self-publish your book. What's more, without a professional publishing team behind you, you'll have to be your own quality controller. Publishers don't necessarily have access to better suppliers than you – it's their high standards and in-depth knowledge of what makes a book look professionally produced that set them apart. This is an important and difficult thing to take into account. I've seen many a self-published book that its author thought looked amazing, but that I could see was 'off'. It can be hard to be objective when you're doing everything yourself, so please treat self-publishing with caution.

However, if you want to go it alone, this is a brief guide to the areas you'll be handling.

Editing
You'll need a copy-editor, a proofreader, and possibly a structural editor as well. Please don't skip these steps, even if they may be the costliest and most time-consuming elements of the process.

Cover design
If you think about how you search for books and decide which ones to buy, you'll realize that the cover design is a critical factor in your decision-making. That's why a professional and experienced cover designer is a must.

Back cover blurb
In a physical store, the blurb on the back cover is the most important element after the cover design and title have been taken into account. And in an online store, your blurb will provide inspiration for the promotional copy in your listing, so it's a critical piece of writing. The blurb should make it clear what your reader's problem is, the solution you offer, and make a promise that the book contains the key to improving their life. You also need to include a short bio that explains what qualifies you to write it, together with a head shot.

People will look at your cover blurb to discover what's in it for them to read your book, and it's probably only *one thing*. I've seen many blurbs that go into too much detail in an attempt to impress potential purchasers, who then end up feeling overwhelmed and confused. If people aren't convinced by it, they won't buy it. What's the 'gold' in your book? Construct your blurb around that.

The technicalities
The barcode on the back of your book encodes its ISBN; it identifies your book to the trade and allows sales tracking to take place. It's not compulsory to have one if you're self-publishing, but it's a good idea because you'll be able to provide verified sales figures if you need them.

Print and upload
In the old days, printing a book meant ordering a couple of thousand copies and stacking them in your garage. Now you can upload your files and have them turned into a professional book that's printed each time a copy is ordered online. Amazon KDP and IngramSpark are the main services for this. If you're publishing an e-book, you can upload the files and cover design onto the online retailers' platforms. In my experience, it's best to have your e-book formatted in the correct file type before you upload it, and to test it before it's published to check that it reads as you expect.

Self-publishing pros
Full control: it's your book, your way. This can be attractive if you have an entrepreneurial mindset and like to move quickly.

Quick and flexible: you can decide when you want your book to appear, and it can be soon.

High royalties: you keep much more of your sales revenue.

Leverage: once your book is out there, you can use it to promote your business however you like.

Self-publishing cons

Lower quality: most authors don't do a great job of creating a professional-looking book because they're not publishing experts. This is the main reason that I hesitate to recommend this route.

Reduced distribution: you don't have an 'in' into the book distributors, so you're limited to selling online and via your own channels. And will you spend time uploading to all the online retailers, or limit yourself to Amazon? Because if it's the latter, you'll be missing out on some sales.

More of your time and energy: you're project managing a process that requires a steep learning curve and is probably only worthwhile if you're planning on writing more than one book (and even then…).

Less prestige: you won't have a known publisher's name on the cover.

Up-front costs: you must pay your suppliers before you make any money from sales (although print-on-demand services reduce the up-front investment).

Lack of marketing support: you're on your own unless you pay someone to help you.

Paid-for publishing

Also called hybrid or partner publishing, this is when you pay a publishing company to publish your book for you. In some ways this gives you the best of both worlds; you don't have the hassle of self-publishing, but you do retain control of your book in a way that you don't with traditional publishing. A helpful way to look at the difference between a paid-for and a traditional publisher is to compare the relationship you have with the two: to a traditional publisher you're a supplier whereas to a paid-for publisher you're a client.

However, choose your publisher wisely. There are many variations in terms of the amount they charge, the royalties they pay, the agreements they ask you to sign, and the distribution they offer. The best are those run by publishing experts who can also give you quality advice on how to position, write, and promote your book – although they may charge extra for that. Speak to several companies and be clear with yourself on what you want to get out of the deal. For instance, if you think that you'll need lots of copies to sell or give away at speaking events, you'll want to know what discount they give on copies you buy for your own use ('author copies'). If getting into traditional bookstores is important to you, some have accounts with wholesalers and some don't. And if you want support with the writing of your book or with marketing and promoting it, you may want to go with a publisher that offers that kind of service.

Any paid-for publisher worth working with will be more than happy to answer your questions, and most offer a free session for you to talk about your book before you commit. It really is one of those areas where the cheapest isn't necessarily the best, so make sure that you feel comfortable about the idea of working with them. They could turn out to be your most valuable supporter when your book is out.

The pros of paid-for publishing
Control and leverage: you get to decide how you want your book to look and, because you retain the copyright, what to do with it once it's published.

Time to market: paid-for publishers work more quickly than traditional publishers, and you don't usually have to wait for them to respond to your proposal.

Expertise: a top-notch publisher will advise you on your options based on what you want to achieve with your book, and they know the industry and its suppliers well.

Distribution: some can get your book into the book distributors or have ways of distributing it abroad.

High royalties: you earn a much higher percentage than with a traditional publisher.

The cons of paid-for publishing

Cost: you pay for the publisher's time, materials, and expertise, so it will cost you more than traditional or self-publishing. You'll also need to pay up front, before you make any money from your book.

Loss of some royalties and copyright compared to self-publishing: depending on the publisher, they may take some of your royalties and/or your copyright for a set period of time. This isn't the case with all, so check.

Marketing support: this is sometimes an extra cost, so while they may advise you on marketing, you might need to pay for it if you want hands-on support (although this is often the case with a traditional publisher too).

I'm a great fan of the paid-for publishing route. It gives you most of the advantages of traditional publishing and avoids the pitfalls inherent in self-publishing. The downside is that it costs you more, but that's the case with many of the best things in life. Naturally it's up to you to decide which to go for, but bear in mind that your book will be around for a long time and will have your name on the cover, so you want it to do you justice.

Book formats

There are three formats that your self-help guide may be consumed in: paperback, e-book, and audio book. It goes without saying that you need the first two (and an e-book is easy to produce in any case, so why not have one?). But what many authors don't consider is having an audio book as well.

Why create an audio book? Because audio is a fast-growing medium. Sales of audio books are still way below print and e-books, but more and more people are buying them. When you think of the popularity of podcasts and the fact that we can carry audio files around with us in our phones, it's not surprising that people are increasingly inclined to listen to books on their commute or while walking the dog. This affords you a new way of accessing people's minds, especially as some people aren't keen on reading anyway.

Creating an audio version of your book might feel like a daunting prospect, but there are specialist companies that can help you. And if you have a publisher, they can almost certainly support you in the task. You can choose whether to narrate your book yourself or hire a professional narrator; the former is more time-consuming but has the advantage that your listeners will hear your own voice. Consider whether your voice is an integral part of your marketing brand. When I created an audio version of my last book, I opted to pay a narrator as I don't do much public speaking or audio marketing, but if I did I'd probably have opted to read it myself.

Now that you understand the publishing landscape, it's time to explore the all-important topic of how you're going to gain a return on your investment from your book. It's the final step of the publishing journey.

The landmarks

- Publishing a book involves many processes, some of which are visible and some of which are not.

- There are three ways of publishing your book: traditional, self, and paid-for.

- Each has its own pros and cons, and the one that I often recommend to self-help authors is paid-for publishing.

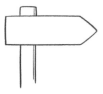

12. Make your book pay

You've come a long way on this journey, so why not set down your suitcase and pause for a moment? You've planned your book, you've written it, you've edited it, and now you're publishing it. You're almost a bona fide, legitimate, genuine author! Who would have thought that was possible on the day when you first sat in front of your screen, wondering where on earth you were going to start and what you were going to say? You have a right to feel proud of yourself.

But there's a piece of the jigsaw missing: how you're going to make this book *worth your while*. I'm sure you've got a lot out of the writing of it already: organizing your thoughts around your expertise, researching your material, and gathering stories and case studies. All of that's of enormous value even if [whispers] *you were never to publish the book*. But what would be the sense in that? You want this book to make a difference, and how will it do that if no one knows about it?

This, folks, is where we talk about marketing. It's where your book starts to pay its way in the world, as well it should.

Marketing isn't a dirty word

In my work as a ghostwriter and book coach I must have conversed with hundreds of coaches, experts and therapists. I find that they can talk forever (sometimes literally) about their area of expertise, but if I mention the word 'marketing' or 'promotion' they stop dead in their tracks. Their smiles drop, their radiance dims, and a despondent look takes over their faces.

'Why can't I just write the book, put it out there and let people read it?' they ask. 'It feels weird to talk about my book to a bunch of people I've never met. How do I find them? What do I say to them? And what if I come across as a self-promotional bore?' To that I say, 'What's the purpose of your book? Is it to languish, unseen and unloved, on a virtual bookshelf? Or is it to help as many people as possible to lead lives of joy and fulfilment – to achieve more, be more, and give more?'

If that's what you want (and I hope you do) your book needs exposure, and lots of it. That's all that marketing is: talking to the right people in the right way about your book.

How to promote your book (and enjoy it)

Hold this thought: might it be possible to *enjoy* promoting your book? And how so? Because it gives you the chance to talk about your favourite subject: your expertise. When you discuss your book in any way, whether it be online, in person, or on stage, what people most want to hear about is what you know. They're not really that interested in your book (yet), but in your knowledge, experience, and passion for your topic. Once you have people hooked on your expertise, you can bring their attention to your book.

This is why marketing your book is a no-fail process, because in the very act of doing it you'll be elevating your expert status, however many copies you do or don't sell. When you talk about your expertise and your book together, they make up more than the sum of their parts; you're the person who 'wrote the book' on it. That's impressive.

So let's dive into how to market your book, with an emphasis on doing it the easy and enjoyable way.

Start early

There's a lot you can do to market your book before you start writing it, let alone publish it. Social media audiences take time to build – you won't gain 1,000 followers overnight. So as soon as you've decided to write a book, think about what channels you want to use to promote it and whether they need any work. Are your LinkedIn connections in need of some care and attention? Have you neglected your Instagram account for a while? Could your website do with a refresh? Now's the time to get them ready for when your book's finished.

Be choosy with your channels

There are many ways to market your book, and it's easy to feel overwhelmed. For this reason, I suggest starting with what you already have. What channels do you already use to promote your work and, of them, which ones bring you the best results? Do you have a blog that you enjoy writing and in which you could publish some extracts from your book? Are you comfortable on stage or on video? Could you build your marketing into your speaking? Do you have an email list that you already use to communicate with current and potential clients, and that you could also employ to give tantalizing previews and pre-publication announcements? It's important to sweat your existing marketing assets rather than to assume that you need new ones.

And if you don't do any marketing for your business already? I'm sorry to be the bearer of bad news, but you need to begin now. You probably have more to start with than you think. What about that Twitter account that's gathering dust? Maybe you have a great network of people who know about your work, but whom you've never formalized into a database? And surely you have a website that you could add a 'book' page to? Once you've done an audit of what you have, you can think about what you want to focus on. There may also be new opportunities that have arisen recently that you've not explored, such as video marketing or the latest social media platform.

Align your audiences

Here's where the strategic planning you did at the beginning comes into its own. Your book marketing needs to have the same audience as your personal development business; if it doesn't, you'll be landing yourself with a lot of extra work – and that's no fun. Aligning your audiences is something that not all self-help authors do, but it's what can make a difference between marketing being a hard slog that delivers few results and it being relatively painless and effective. For instance, if you help people in mid-life to find new partners, make sure that your book is aimed at those in that age group. It sounds obvious, but it's easily forgotten when you're in the throes of creating a marketing plan for your book.

Marketing channels

You may have heard people talking about 'marketing channels', and all they mean is the range of methods you can use to reach your potential book buyers. Here I'll outline the main offline and online channels so that you can see what your options are. Please don't feel that you should work with them all – in fact, try not to. Using your knowledge of what already works for you, choose two or three to focus on and leave the rest.

Offline marketing

This is any kind of marketing that doesn't involve sitting in front of a screen. That may make it irresistibly attractive to you, or it may not. The advantages are that you don't need to master any tech stuff for it, and if you're used to doing business face to face it probably feels comfortable for you. The downside is that there are only so many people you can interact with offline – it has an inherent limitation.

Here are the main offline channels that you could use to promote your book.

PR in print, TV, and radio
This can take different forms: media articles, interviews, book reviews, and TV and radio interviews. While many authors jump at the chance to be interviewed about their book on these media, they don't tend to sell many books as a result. That's because offline media tends to be consumed away from the most convenient place to buy your book, which is on a computer or other device. Your listeners or readers can't click on a link and be taken straight to an online bookstore – they must remember to do it later (with predictable results).

The best way of making use of offline media is as a platform to promote your expertise, rather than to sell your book. You may have noticed how often chat show guests have just published a book; in other words, the book is their excuse to talk to a journalist or interviewer about what they do. You can use it for that, too.

What do you need in order to generate some PR? All journalists want an angle, preferably a topical one. As a self-help author, you're ideally placed for this. If you're an alcohol recovery coach and a previously sober celebrity has just landed themselves in trouble after falling off the wagon, this is your opportunity to talk about the ongoing support people need if they're to maintain their sobriety. Or if you specialize in helping teenagers to cope with anxiety and depression, and there's a big news article about the harmful effects of social media on that generation, you can base your advice on that. The more up to date, controversial, emotion-driven, and personal your angle is, the better. I recommend the book *Make Yourself a Little Bit Famous* by Penny Haslam for advice on how to contact the media and present yourself in interviews.

Speaking
Being both an author and a speaker is a bit like strawberries and cream – they go together in the best possible way. Not only can your book give you structured content for your talks, but you'll also be far more attractive to a speaker booker once you're an author. One of my ghostwriting clients told me that he was able to double his speaking fees once his book was published.

So, if you're a speaker – whether professional or occasional – how can you use your talks to promote your book? One way is to sell copies of it at the events you speak at; some speakers even negotiate a certain number of copies to be bought as part of their fee. Another is always to be thinking about how you can bring your book into your speaking. The next time you're filmed doing a talk, make sure that you hold your book up to the audience, and then insert footage of this into your showreel. Or how about being interviewed on your book topic for a series of videos? Through this you'll build your book into the marketing you're already doing for your speaking career.

Also, whenever you receive a booking enquiry, send the person a copy of your book. This will give them a feel for your tone of voice and approach so that they have the chance to know, like, and trust you before you've even met. A tip one professional speaker gave me is to put a sticky note on the cover suggesting the most relevant chapter for them to look at, given the topic of the talk they're suggesting.

Online marketing

The great thing about promoting your book online is that every message you put out has the potential to be seen by thousands of people – and you don't even have to leave the house. The downside is that if you can do it, so can everyone else. This means you must create a strong online identity for yourself. Offline, you can get away with being somewhat generalized about what you do because you have the chance to build face-to-face relationships that make you memorable ('I'm a career coach'), but in the online space you're afforded no such luxury. If your potential readers aren't instantly grabbed by your compelling marketing message, your competitors' books are only a click away. Instead of 'I'm a career coach', it should be, 'I help recent graduates to find the work that lights them up – and I've written a book about it as well.'

Here are some ways to carve out a niche for yourself in internet-land.

Your website

I'm assuming that you already have a website for your business, and rarely is there a need to create a separate one for your book. In fact, it's usually better to promote your book on your existing site, so that each supports the other. People viewing your website will be doubly convinced of your authority: not only are you showcasing your expertise on there, but it's clear that you've written a book about it too.

You can create a new page on your site to feature your book. Include a picture of the cover, who it's for, what unique and timely advice or information it offers, and the knowledge that your potential readers will gain from reading it. How will their lives be different? What's in it for them? This is also the place to include a link to buy it.

However, the value of your website doesn't stop at promoting your book. You can also use it to give your readers extra resources, thereby bolstering the value of the book for them. If you 'gate' these resources behind an email sign-up form, you have the bonus of being able to carry on an online conversation long term.

Your blog

A personal development guide is a bit like a huge, structured blog. Both are geared towards a specific audience, both impart useful and inspiring information, and both aim to change their readers' lives for the better. The main differences are that a blog does this in bite-sized chunks and is updateable after publication, whereas a book delivers the whole thing in one go and is 'forever'. It follows from this that your blog is an ideal place to promote your book, and also that by writing your book you've already generated a lot of the blog content you need.

There are many ways to approach writing a blog post. Try these ideas:

- Write posts based on your book's content, mentioning the book at the end with a link to buy it.

- Interview an expert with complementary expertise to your own and mention your book at the end.

- Create a controversial post that highlights your unique take on your subject and build your book into that.

- Film a series of videos talking about various elements of your book, hosting them on your video channel of choice and embedding them into your blog.

Your email list

If you already send a regular email to your target audience, it makes obvious sense to use it to market your book – however small the list. You can also generate excitement at launch and encourage longer-term sales by including your book in your email footer and mentioning it strategically every now and then. Even just telling your recipients that you've written a book will be a credibility builder in its own right; you'll probably see a surge in sales of your services along with those for your book.

Social media

This is one of those areas that there are so many things to love about, and so many things to hate. Which camp do you fall into? If you don't want to get involved there's no need to force yourself, but you'll be shutting off a lot of valuable opportunities if you do. Why not read on and see whether you change your mind?

An important point about social media: it's not a quick fix. You need to spend time attracting followers, engaging with them, and posting content that's useful and interesting before you see results. This can take several months at a minimum. The following assumes that you've already built a presence or are willing to spend time on doing so.

Mainstream social media for the self-help market is currently made up of these platforms: Twitter, Instagram, Facebook, LinkedIn, YouTube, and TikTok. Of course, by the time you read this it's possible that another social network will have sprung up, but for now these are the main ones. Drawing on my previous experience as a social media manager for businesses, here are some top-line tips for how you could use social media to market your book:

- Add 'author of...' to your profile description.
- Include your book in your profile header image.
- Build pre-publication anticipation by asking for feedback on your book cover design choices.
- Create posts to announce your book's publication, with a link to where people can buy it.
- Post about the main topics in your book, linking to your book's page on your website (or where it's sold online) at the end.
- Create images out of key book quotes and post them.
- For video channels, film yourself talking about why you wrote the book and what's in it for your readers, adding a link to buy it high up in the video description.
- Create a series of videos based on different chapters of your book.

Podcast interviews

It can't have escaped your notice that the number of podcasts has exploded in recent years. It seems as if everyone has taken to the mic, and while this means that there are a lot of short-lived and mediocre podcasts out there, there are also an increasing amount of high-quality ones that would be well worth you being interviewed on. Some of them have large tribes of loyal listeners.

If being grilled on a podcast sounds a bit scary, please don't be put off. Most are recorded on an audio-only basis, so all you have to think about is what you say and how you sound, not how you look. And your host will want to put you at your ease so that the interview is an enjoyable experience for their listeners – it's in everyone's interests for you to feel relaxed. What's more, a podcast is an excellent way of positioning yourself as the go-to authority on your topic and can link beautifully with promoting your book. I've appeared on multiple podcasts over the years and can testify to their effectiveness in gaining exposure; several clients have mentioned that they first heard of me when they listened to me on a podcast.

Just make sure that the podcast audience is similar to that for your book. For instance, if you help people to build exercise into their daily routine, you'll want to be interviewed on a fitness or diet-related podcast. Also, make sure that you take advantage of the opportunity by basing your answers on your book's topic as much as you can. It's easy to be sucked into just having a fun chat and at the end realize that you haven't mentioned your book or its content at all. Try to ensure that the podcast host has read your book before the interview; you won't always succeed, but when you do you'll find that the discussion revolves around your book much more effectively.

And finally, the show should have episode notes where you can include your bio, so include a link to your book there.

Hybrid channels

There are a couple of channels that have been thriving across both online and offline interfaces for many years now: support groups, and webinars and workshops.

Support groups

When you're writing about a topic that helps people, there are almost certainly numerous support groups based around it. They can be in person or online, and the brilliant thing about them for your book is that they provide a ready-made market for it. Why not visit those groups? If they're online, you can drop by with helpful comments and advice, mentioning your book if it seems relevant (as long as that's within the group guidelines). And if you're able to visit in-person groups, you can give a talk based on your book's content. You need to be careful not to come across as salesy, but if you focus first and foremost on how you can help people it will naturally lead to people being interested in your book.

Maybe you can even run a support group yourself. One of my clients managed a popular Facebook group for people with drug dependency issues, and the platform that this gave him was instrumental in him gaining a traditional publisher for his book. It also generated a wealth of material to use for the book, including positive testimonials and quotations from engaged members. He hadn't intended the group to be beneficial in this way when he first started – all he'd originally wanted was to support people who had the same problem as him – but as is often the way, helping others can lead to good things happening to yourself.

Webinars and workshops

In many ways, these are online and offline versions of each other. Both are designed to give people information in digestible and engaging ways, and both can involve a certain amount of participant interaction. Hosting a series of these could be an excellent way to showcase your book's content and generate sales. You could even hold an exclusive event to reward people who've helped you with your book in some way: beta readers, people who've promoted it for you, and anyone who's contributed through offering their views and support.

A final note

When you're thinking about how you're going to market your book and make a return on your investment, it's easy to overlook the fact that your 'profit' won't necessarily equate to the numbers of copies you sell. For a start, royalties are usually slim, even if you self-publish; you'd have to sell a *lot* of books to make any significant income from them alone. *Who* you sell the book to is more important than how many copies you shift. I made an early return on my investment with my last book when I gained a client who had found it online, read it, liked it, and decided to work with me on that basis. Of course, we all want to sell lots of books, but it's not the only target to aim at.

The landmarks

- If you want your book to make a difference, you need to promote it to many potential readers.
- Marketing your book can be fun and relatively simple – it doesn't have to be an onerous task.
- Offline channels include PR and speaking.
- Online channels include your website, your blog, email, social media, and podcasts.

- There are also hybrid channels such as support groups, webinars, and workshops.

The end or the beginning?

You've reached the end of your journey into self-help book authorship. Or have you? In the same way as I've been your guide throughout this book, you're going to be the leading light for your readers in yours. Stepping into that role can prompt you to think about what you do in new ways, and you may find yourself discovering frameworks and analogies that work better for your clients than those you use now. In that sense, writing your book is only the beginning of the next phase of your career.

Which is great, but how do you galvanize yourself to write a book and keep going until it's finished? In *Big Magic*, Elizabeth Gilbert advises her readers to 'create whatever causes a revolution in your heart'. She's advocating writing about what moves you and gives you pleasure, because by doing that you'll produce something meaningful for your readers as well as for yourself. In other words, have some fun. Writing a transformational book isn't all about hard work, it's also about tapping into what inspires you to do the work that you do. If you know what that is, you're part way towards writing a successful book already.

However, becoming and staying inspired isn't always easy. In fact, sometimes it's damn hard. That's why I like to keep a couple of books on my desk that I know will give me something to aspire to. They're like my mentors, showing me that it's possible to write a guide that's enjoyable, motivating, and pure of purpose. I suggest that you do the same. Who's written books that you look up to as being shining examples of what you want to achieve? Why not dip into them throughout your writing journey, using them as supplementary guides to this one?

And finally, persist. It doesn't matter how brilliant your ideas are, how effectively you write about them, the volume of knowledge and experience you have, and how much you love the idea of the finished book – if you don't keep going, you won't arrive at your destination. That doesn't mean you have to keep pushing yourself when you don't feel like it, but it does mean that it's worth finding out *why* you don't feel like it. Maybe you need to revisit your structure or format to see whether it's still working for you – that can be the cause of a lot of 'stuckness'. Another reason might be that you're not sure what you're trying to say in a given chapter, in which case it's worth spending some time getting clear before you go any further. Or maybe you just need a break. That's fine – there are no medals for finishing a book in a set number of months. You'll need plenty of fuel in the tank when it comes to promoting your book, so it doesn't make sense to use it all up while you're writing it.

One thing's for sure, writing a self-help book is a journey on which both you and your readers will learn all sorts of new and fascinating things. And it's one that gives you entry into the 'published author club', a space well worth joining. I hope that this guide has given you all the advice and support you need to send you on your way. Bon voyage!

The author

Ginny Carter is a non-fiction book ghostwriter and coach. She's ghostwritten over 25 books about a variety of topics, from career development to entrepreneurship to communication skills. These books have two things in common: they're helping their readers to improve their lives and they're bringing their authors visibility and authority in their fields.

Ginny is also the author of the award-winning *Your Business Your Book*, which takes you through the key steps for planning, writing, and promoting a business book. She's a judge for the Business Book Awards, and as a keen blogger, she gives advice and support to authors through her website (details below).

When she can be dragged away from her keyboard, Ginny enjoys country walks, travelling to interesting places, and sessions in the gym (well, kind of). Other times, she'll be found with her nose in a book.

If you have a book waiting to emerge but aren't sure where to begin or whether you have the time to devote to it, please start a conversation by dropping her a line using one of the links below:

Website: www.marketingtwentyone.co.uk

LinkedIn: www.linkedin.com/in/ginnycarter

Twitter: @_GinnyCarter

Acknowledgements

First, thank you to the people who read this book in manuscript form before it was published and gave me invaluable feedback and advice. Grace Marshall, Ishy Bruce, Alison Jones – I'm grateful for your time and expertise.

Thank you also to the team at Practical Inspiration for turning my manuscript into a living, breathing, published book. It's way more exciting to hold the real thing than to look at a document on a screen.

And finally, my gratitude to the coaches, therapists, and trainers around the world who dedicate their time and energy to transforming people's lives for the better. It's these 'helpers' whom so many of us have to thank for the health and happiness we enjoy.

Index